HOPE IN ALL THINGS
but shhh, keep the secrets safe

DR. CATHY KIRKLAND & DR. TODD KIRKLAND

HOPE IN ALL THINGS
but shhh, keep the secrets safe

 LUCIDBOOKS

Hope in ALL Things
Copyright © 2022 by Cathy Kirkland & Todd Kirkland

Published by Lucid Books in Houston, TX
www.LucidBooks.com

All rights reserved. No part of this publication may be reproduced, stored in a retrieval system, or transmitted in any form by any means, electronic, mechanical, photocopy, recording, or otherwise, without the prior permission of the publisher, except as provided for by USA copyright law.

Scripture quotations marked (NIV) are taken from the Holy Bible, New International Version®, NIV®. Copyright ©1973, 1978, 1984, 2011 by Biblica, Inc.™ Used by permission of Zondervan. All rights reserved worldwide. www.zondervan.com The "NIV" and "New International Version" are trademarks registered in the United States Patent and Trademark Office by Biblica, Inc.™

eISBN: 978-1-63296-572-1
ISBN: 978-1-63296-600-1

Special Sales: Most Lucid Books titles are available in special quantity discounts. Custom imprinting or excerpting can also be done to fit special needs. Contact Lucid Books at Info@LucidBooks.com

*For our daughter, Hannah.
You are the miracle that God gave us.*

TABLE OF CONTENTS

Backstory 1

Chapter One – The Road Ahead 5

Chapter Two – Pain.. 13

Chapter Three – The Crew 23

Chapter Four – The Fabulous Four? 33

Chapter Five – Safe? 39

Chapter Six – Letters... 51

Chapter Seven – Thankful?... 55

Chapter Eight – Hope 69

Chapter Nine – Heart Exposed 79

Chapter Ten – Jesus Freak 93

Chapter Eleven – Mat 99

Chapter Twelve – Protection 105

Chapter Thirteen – Extra Blankets 111

Chapter Fourteen – Dear Caleb 117

Chapter Fifteen – Confession 133

Epilogue... 143

Acknowledgments 145

BACKSTORY

More than twenty years ago, we were given the sad news that having children of our own would not be possible. We reluctantly accepted the news and decided to help other parents love their children well. We felt that being a blessing would be better than dwelling on our own sadness and closing off our hearts.

This led us to research foster care in hopes of adopting a child. Finally, we were asked to foster a five-year-old who had been diagnosed with severe reactive attachment disorder. We said yes because we naively believed that love could conquer all. But life would teach us many unwanted lessons through the difficult journey of trying to reach a reactive attachment child. We learned that normal logic and parenting do not apply; unfortunately, some of these children are damaged and shaped by severe and systematic abuse. For three years we tried to work with Philip and hoped to adopt him, but God said no. Love was not enough in Philip's case, and the State moved in and locked him away in an institution. We were devastated and could not understand God's seeming cruelty; there were so many confusing and devastating moments during this time.

As a distraction from our pain, this book was birthed. We used the storytelling process to help take our minds off our pain. Then after the manuscript was completed, we placed it in a trunk along with sad reminders of our foster child's existence. We were not convinced that this manuscript should ever see the light of day. The story deals with topics that were rarely spoken about in churches back then even though evils such as child abuse were not uncommon. Fortunately, people are becoming more aware of the damage caused by child abuse and hard life decisions that have eternal consequences like the events in this story.

Our foster child was a broken product of the kind of lasting scars inflicted on children by adults who are either trying to cause pain or who have a skewed idea of what love really is. How can anyone deliberately hurt a child? Sadly, too many do so every day. Many adults hurt children without remorse, and worse yet, some do so and try to call their actions "justifiable" even though we know those are merely lies.

We dedicate this book to everyone who has ever been scarred by abuse—especially to those who were innocent children. To you, we say, "It was not your fault. No one deserves abuse. With God, your story's ending can be masterfully woven into something useful and good. Yes, even from abuse. It was not God's will for you to be abused." God was screaming in the adults' numbed consciousness, but they refused to hear and obey. That is the hard side of freedom of choice; the broken mind can choose the evil it wants.

To illustrate this point, our foster child's story did not have a perfect ending. As a young child, he had no choice, and he just needed safe people around him. However, as he grew, he had his own choices to make, and he fell by them as anyone with his life experience could. But we cannot overemphasize this message: if someone is abused, it does not give them license to live in self-destruction. For evil to end, someone must stop it in their generation—swearing that it will not pass through them.

Even with the tragedy we experienced, our story is still amazing. After twenty years of waiting, God opened my womb once and only once in my lifetime. We were blessed with a beautiful surprise baby girl when I was forty-six and my husband was forty-eight. Yes, we are something of a modern-day Abraham and Sarah. Our lives are full, and we help others find healing from brokenness through our counseling practice, Beautifully Broken Counseling (Murfreesboro, Tennessee).

After this story lay hiding in the trunk for many years, we allowed our good friends Ross and Dana to read the rough draft. They were both moved and urged us to look into the possibility of publishing it. We found that Lucid Books was willing to partner with us on this project and after all those years, we feel blessed to share this story with the world.

We pray that our story will give hope to all those scarred by abuse and loss. We want our readers to feel inspired to not give up, but to . . . *Hope in ALL Things*.

****

If you have been hurt by abuse and want to break free, we can help nationwide. See our website for a Patient Intake Form.

www.beautifullybrokencounseling.com

CHAPTER ONE
The Road Ahead

"Hurry up, Joy; you're going to be late again!" said Joy's editor, Mr. Stanley. Joy was rushing as fast as her small frame and thinly veiled body would allow her to travel. She had only thirty minutes to get to the airport on time for her departure to Charlotte, North Carolina.

"I just cannot miss another one. Failure to get this story is not an option." Joy could always be found talking to herself as if she were scolding an employee.

She had missed two of her last five assignments, which did not reflect her drive to be a top-notch journalist. She was not considered a first-rate choice among journalists because she always went after the types of stories that had to do with some prominent church leader who had fallen from grace as it were. Joy clung to the belief that one day she would discover the one big story that would shake the religious world to its very core. The thought of such vindication forced her to move forward to the next lead like a soldier going to the front lines of battle. And this most recent lead, she thought with anticipation, might just be the story to end all stories. She had received a tip that in Asheville, North Carolina, there was a ring of porn-peddlers who had been using a local church as a front—they were ministers, in fact, men of the cloth who supposedly had a calling from God.

Joy began to talk out loud to herself saying, "How in the world could anyone be so cruel and without conscience as to use children as objects to fulfill the desires of sick, perverted, and even possessed men and women? Even worse, how could men who were called by God to protect these innocent young lives be the ones who were the perpetrators?"

As she was filled with disgust at the thought of all the little children's hearts that would forever be scarred, Joy felt sick over the memories that these thoughts brought back to her mind and heart. She fought daily to keep her own inner scars squelched by a constant flurry of activity. Her scars were fashioned in her heart by her very own father, also a religious leader. But as quickly as the thoughts came, she had always been able to ram them back down into her soul to be dealt with at a later day, a day that she secretly hoped would never come. So, she decidedly forced herself to change the subject.

Joy settled her mind on the original intention for her trip to North Carolina. She could not be sure of anything except the drive that would push her on to find the truth. It is not that she found it hard to believe that "religious" men were doing horrible things in Asheville. She had been privy to the first disclosures of a denomination and its problems resulting from years of sexual molestation. There was unbelievable, yet undeniable evidence of a cover-up that had gone on for years with the church moving ministers from parish to parish. Still, even if she were wrong about this latest lead, she could use the time away from the office (as well as away from what was going on in her personal life) to re-focus her thoughts and feelings and sort them out. So, she found herself looking forward to the journey as well as the hunt. Or in other words, this would give her time to, "Just be."

When Joy arrived in Charlotte, the attendant behind the automobile rental counter asked, "Did you have a good flight, Miss?" "I think so," Joy said, amazed that she had slept through a large portion of the flight. She did not want to remember her dream, the one dream that seemed to come to her when she was under real stress. As Joy signed the rental forms for a 2003 Chrysler Sebring convertible, she realized that she was eagerly looking forward to the drive with the car's top down. It was an amazingly beautiful day, the kind that had those feather-weight clouds in which children always see faces—the kind that adults have long since lost the innocence or patience to take notice of. The backdrop of blue appeared as if the ocean itself were hanging behind the clouds. As she started the car and put the top down, a breeze of peace entered Joy's soul and begged her to believe that, maybe soon, her unrelenting problems and sleep-stealing dreams would be moving along like the clouds, being pushed away by the gentle, calm wind.

After leaving the airport, Joy decided that she needed to make a quick stop at a convenience store for a drink. Noticing the first sign on the freeway for such a stop, she pulled over and went in. Trying to think of anything she might need for this short trip, such as tissues, a map, snacks, and drinks, she caught herself smiling at her incessant need to be prepared for anything that may come her way. She did not like to be controlled by circumstances, anyone, or anything.

"Come on Joy," she gently chided herself, "this is a two-hour drive. Just enjoy it." She hurriedly checked her items out at the counter, continued to the car, got in, put the key in the ignition, and started her engine. Just as she was getting ready to put the car in reverse, she stopped.

She noticed the map she had bought peeking at her as it was balanced on top of her newly purchased items. Then she thought about what she had just told herself, "Come on, Joy; just enjoy the journey."

Taking the map out of the bag and unfolding it, she began looking for a less traveled road that she could drive so she could just take in the scenery as she headed to her destination. After all, she had hurried to make the flight out of Chicago, and now there was no real reason to be rushed since her crew would not be arriving at the hotel until later that day.

Her crew members were "wrapping up" another story in Virginia that dealt with a supposed murder-suicide of a local minister and a disgruntled church member. This unexpected extra time allowed Joy to cherry-pick the road that appeared to be the most adventurous and remote.

She pulled out onto the freeway heading west on I-85; then she would take exit 153 and reward herself with a much-needed entrance to a slower pace, if only for an hour or so.

After only thirty minutes on I-85, she noticed her exit up ahead. Another half a mile and she would be there, yet she could not be more annoyed at the car in front of her, which had already begun slowing down to exit at the same ramp. Joy never allowed herself to be cornered, so she pulled onto the left lane. She gunned the accelerator, racing past the turtle as she played the rabbit to arrive at the exit first. Coming to the top of the ramp, she turned right on Highway 211 heading northwest. As the road began to open up, it was as if the road itself were inviting her for a dance, and she graciously acquiesced with a blush. A few more miles into the journey, she began to relax somewhat and turned on the radio, trying to find a jazz station. She loved jazz—something about the way it just spontaneously came together.

After multiple unsuccessful searches for local jazz options, she felt defeated and settled on an easy-listening station instead.

Feeling her body stiffening with a semi-stretch and yawn, she began to think about the story and how she would begin to unleash her journalistic skills on this small band of so-called "men of God."

"Men of God?" she questioned in her mind with an outward smirk of disgust on her face. "Who even knows what that means?"

Joy had seen enough phonies in her short career to know that everyone has skeletons in their closets. It is just that some closets are very small and much harder to hide secrets in, and others are walk-ins, large enough to hide things better amidst the clutter of sinful lives lived in secret. Rehearsing in her mind as the dance continued, she began to relish the conquest of the past battles in which she had played a role. Like sorting through a filing cabinet and lifting a file labeled with a particular name or heading, she could pull up the files from memory, relishing each one in her mind and reliving them all over again. With a gleeful grin, she remembered a preacher's wife in Florida. Joy had played a pivotal role in exposing the minister's wife. The good pastor's wife was an embezzler. So much so that she had run up high loan tabs during her dance with a gambling circuit. This in turn led the pastor's wife, who was also working as the part-time church secretary, to defraud the church. And of course, with Joy's ability to find the story behind the story, she was able to discover that the pastor was a willing participant in the cover-up. Closing that file, she at once opened another one.

This file was of special importance to Joy because she had firsthand knowledge related to it. This particular file always produced a "Grinch-like" snarl in her. And although this attitude was directly in contrast to the meaning of her name, Joy, it nonetheless caused her certain feelings of joy in the satisfaction of exposing another so-called "man of God." She recalled the youth leader of a large metropolitan church in an urban setting who had been sentenced to twenty-five years in prison. Joy had helped the police discover that the local rumors about the man were much more than just rumors. They were true stories of young men and women who had been scarred by the perverted and ungodly behavior of this minister. Young people had at first come to the minister seeking help with the usual problems that teenagers encounter. And then, as if matters could not be any worse surrounding this drama, Joy once again uncovered the story behind the story. She discovered evidence that the church's senior pastor knew of the rumors and the hidden truths. Then he tried to use the media to help him convince the public that the church was in no way liable for the actions of this junior minister. The senior pastor was trying to avoid any lawsuits for negligence or to settle out of court. He obviously was more worried about the size of his paycheck than the deep and abiding screams of "Why?" that could be heard coming from the hurting children who were encamped outside his "ivory palace." However, it was a palace that would prove to be built on sand and when the dust settled, it was discovered that the molester had three years earlier moved from another state where similar accusations had been made against him.

Joy saw this as her service to mankind: to expose these "Prophets of Baal" as her father used to refer to them. These men were "prophets" who were so perverted and fallen in their hearts that they would sacrifice their very own children on the altar of Baal to feed their wicked and driven passions.

Joy was obviously relishing the mind game of replaying past triumphs, but she wanted to stop for a while and get out of the car and look at the beautiful mountains. Pulling over at the nearest overlook, she got out of the car and took a deep cleansing breath of the pure, crisp mountain air.

As she savored the beauty of the autumn colors painted on the landscape of treetops, she asked herself, "How could something so beautiful as this world, be so ugly as to contain the sick-hearted humans that I have frequently encountered in my short, but relatively hard life?"

The flaming colors of orange, yellow, and red caused her to recall a Scripture from her childhood days in Miss Epps's Sunday school class; Miss Epps was the kindest woman Joy had ever known. The Scripture from Romans explained how God is always speaking to us through the beauty of the things that He has made for us. Thinking on this and her memories of Miss Epps's kindness caused her to ask the obvious question: "Is there really a God? And if there is, where was He when I was hurt? Where is He now when so many children are so incredibly in need of a mighty hero to rescue them?" In deep despair of heart, she wanted to believe. It was as if she wanted God Himself to audibly answer her from the beautiful blue sky. But wanting to believe and see the truth to believe were two different animals altogether.

Therefore, with a mixed heart as always, she resolved that these questions might forever go unanswered, and to the mind of a reporter, that was simply not an acceptable choice. Joy was committed to continuing to do her part to search for the truth, no matter where it led and who may be hung by their craftily disguised lies.

Returning to her car, Joy continued her drive and resumed her file game of past successes. These memories were in no small way helping fuel the flames for the next conquest that lay ahead of her. She was becoming more and more confident with each passing memory that filled her with delight and pride regarding all she had done to expose those who hide behind God for cover. There were moments when she was very concerned over her thrill, and almost blood lust when perusing these assignments. No doubt she enjoyed, maybe lived for, these adventures, especially when the possible outcome would be another folder to place in her great file of proof that what the world needs more than love is good, old-fashioned righteous indignation. She felt people with this sort of determination are more doers than people who just sit around and contemplate what heaven will be like for them, and "to hell" with the rest of us.

There was just something deliciously satisfying about giving these so-called "religious" types their "just rewards." Still, some leads did not pan out, and she had not always found what she searched for, despite her dogged diligence.

There was more than one story over the years that she could not crack. And of course, that is exactly how Joy interpreted those unsuccessful outcomes. It never crossed her mind that some of the tips she received had proven to be unsubstantiated because the accused were innocent. No! She was always convinced that every tip was a legitimate fact that just needed some true grit and a lucky break or two to uncover the seething lies that had been hidden under the canopy of religion. Therefore, she did not like to think about those times when she was forced to admit that she could have been wrong about anything. Her dogmatic approach might have come from her father and his stern regard for his rules: Rule One – he was always right; and Rule Two – when in doubt, refer back to rule number one. Although she hated to admit any common ground with her father, she had to acknowledge that she was just like him when it came to her refusal to face the reality that she just might be wrong on a few occasions—but only on a very few occasions.

She chuckled to herself as she thought of her father in the happier times when these two rules were more of a joke to him than a philosophy of life. In those days, she quietly sighed, "It was fun being my daddy's little girl."

Just then, a tear came to her eye as she remembered the sweet days. But she quickly was thrust back into the reality that those "sweet days" will forever be stolen by the memories surrounding the loss of her sweet baby girl. What type of father chooses self-righteousness, and control over his own daughter and grandchild? She answered herself with anger: "The type that would rather choose a cover-up than help his daughter raise her own daughter." Joy's protective hard shell quickly surrounded her heart to protect her from falling apart. This hard covering had served her well to keep her sane, but it had done nothing for her love life except pushing away everyone who had ever tried to get close to her. Nonetheless, she hated to be wrong, and she was afraid that dwelling on past failures would only serve to force her into a breakdown of her psyche and cause her to question her abilities as an investigative reporter. For if she admitted she was mistaken, it could only mean one of two things: she was either wrong in her assumptions, or she was not as "top-notch" a reporter as she would like to believe. Still, some cases will always be troubling to her.

As she often did, Joy began to speak to herself as a mother giving a child a pep talk at the end of an exhausting day at school. "Joy! Now that is enough of the pity party. Get your mind back on the present, and always remember: one, you are always right and two, when in doubt, refer back to rule number one." Her spirit was lifted, and she began to enjoy the journey again.

"Oh, no!" As instinct took over, she hammered the brakes trying to reach the bottom of the floorboard with the brake pedal. Cutting across the oncoming lane and then bouncing off a wall back across to the other side, with tires screaming as burning rubber glided across the asphalt, she felt the car going over the embankment. Heading down the embankment nose first, the car came to a terrible and sudden stop with the force of a sledgehammer. The force catapulted her head against the inflating airbag, simultaneously tossing her head to the left like a rubber ball.

CHAPTER TWO
Pain

Pain . . . a throbbing pain running through her whole body, telling her that all was not right. Coming too slowly, she tried to open her eyes and get them to focus. Everything was a blur at first; then, she slipped back into unconsciousness. Hours later, she awoke again remembering what had caused the accident and the terror that gripped her more than the pain that was still racking her head and her body. Looking down toward her chest, she could see bloodstains that had already dried into a crimson color of spatters and drops across her shirt like the art canvas of a modern impressionistic painter. She felt the seat belt that was harnessing her body give way as she pushed the latch button on the buckle. She slumped over into the now deflated airbag.

Reaching for the door handle that she hoped would allow her to make a much-needed exit from the car, she soon discovered that she could not push the door open. The car had landed nose-first into the embankment crushing the front exterior like an empty can of cola. Because the door panels were compressed, she could not exit via the normal route. Joy pulled herself up from the bucket seat and crawled out over the door panel, landing on the mud below. Breathing as if her body had just endured a marathon, she felt her body was too weak to receive any commands from her will to get up and move.

While lying on her back with her face up toward the sky, she noticed for the first time that daylight was closing onto the oncoming night. Her mind reeled: "How long have I been out here like this, and why hadn't anyone come to help?" The most pressing question haunting her was whether or not she had hit the little girl. This startled her mind and strengthened her body as adrenaline flowed through her veins like a raging river in search of the wide-open ocean. She almost leapt up, as the question of the little girl's safety became the priority.

Climbing up the steep hillside as if she were climbing out of her own intended grave, every move stabbed her with pain like a knife into her flesh. She reached the road. With amazement, she sighed the sound of great relief as her visual investigation could not find the small girl's body. She thought it very strange: there was nothing around the black tire marks or even alongside the parallel lines of the road's edges.

"What could have happened to her?" Joy questioned.

She began to rationalize that maybe a rescue team had come and rushed the little girl to a hospital. She continued to question, but as quickly as she thought of that scenario, she brushed it aside as impossible. "If that were true, how could they have been so inept as to have missed my car?" From her standing position on the road, she glanced over toward the car's vicinity and could not see even the taillights. The only visible remains from the accident were the black tire marks that looked like two parallel snakes slithering away into the grassy edges of the road.

Maybe someone came along and found the little girl on the road and took her to safety. Again though, she pondered, "Why had no one found me in the ditch?" Canvassing the immediate area before all daylight was extinguished, she could not see any remnant of blood, clothing, or personal belongings that would indicate someone had been struck by a car. She wondered to herself, "How could this be?" She knew what she had seen. But still, where could the little girl have come from so suddenly? Joy was on a particularly long and straight stretch of highway. She was not an irresponsible driver. She did not see the child approaching the road from the outer edges. It was as if the child just suddenly appeared from out of nowhere.

Then a thought came to her—that she needed to help herself. She began to limp over to the road's edge to get back down to the car. Carefully maneuvering the sloping landscape, she began to slide down the wall of the embankment as her body began tumbling until it found its resting place beside the car's passenger door. Gripping the top of the doorframe and pulling herself up to view, she found her purse open, and all its contents littered throughout the inside of the car.

She spoke out loud, hoping that someone might answer her and she would find that she was not completely alone. "Where is my phone?"

She needed help since this was a back road where evidently few people traveled. Her phone would be her only source of comfort. As the minutes, which seemed like hours, ticked by, she could not locate the phone. Then, as if a firefly had appeared, she caught a glimpse of the evening light reflecting off the metallic casing of her phone. It was only a few feet away, and she reached toward it like a thirsty man running to receive a cold drink. She fell toward it and grabbed the phone like a lifeline. As she picked it up, she could see it had been destroyed. The back was hanging from the face of the phone; most of the wires were snapped in two, and there were only a couple of wires left to hold the two pieces together.

"Please, please, please work!" Joy begged.

Against all hope, she tried to activate the phone's charge by continually pushing down the power button. Joy longed for the two miracles of light and sound on her phone both of which usually annoyed her, but she thought they would be like heaven on earth at this very moment. But there was only silence and darkness. As her strength from adrenaline had been deflated, so was the hope in her heart and mind that she was going to get help. She felt herself fall to the ground and once again slipped away into the realm of the unconscious.

Descending into an exhausted sleep, Joy's mind began to replay the dream that always caused her to wake with regret and resentment. Only this time, her body was too tired to allow her to resist the final chapter of the dream. It was as if she could see all the past events played on a large screen as though she had been tied to a chair and forced to watch the horror and the pain:

The cold, insensitive metal stirrups upon her calves and feet felt like pins of icicles, which soon warmed to her body heat. The doctor, aided by nurses wearing masks, made the "procedure" seem so impersonal. As she lay there, she could not believe her father would approve of such a thing—much less demand it of his own daughter. He was a deacon in the church and had always said that this kind of thing was murder. Yet now she was being forced to cooperate with his wishes to save the so-called family from being dishonored. *Honor*, she thought, what a hypocritical word. How could anyone have honor and integrity and insist on such a ghastly act as this, and she was only seventeen. She knew that becoming pregnant before marriage was wrong, and she was willing to put the baby up for adoption, but not this.

Joy began to question herself, "Why am I going along with it? How will this affect my life from now on?"

It appears that *honor* was a word that was imposed upon others to do the "right" thing. But now that it had come to her family, she had clearly received the message that reputation and social standing with the "good church folk" were obviously more vital than whether or not a murder was about to be committed. She felt that the wrongs that can be swept under the carpet and kept hidden in the shadows seemed to be the choice of the "good" people of the church rather than open honesty.

Her mind reeled. "But how could my father demand the sacrifice of my child? My first child? His grandchild? Brad's child?"

As the dream continued, she very desperately wished she could wake up. Again, her body would not allow it.

She began to dream more deeply: "Brad's child?"

She had told Brad about the pregnancy. At first, he was shocked with disbelief. As time went on, he said he would stand by whatever decision she made. He said he did not feel that they should have to get married but would do whatever he could do to support her baby, his baby!

Brad had been a star football player in high school. It was there that they had met and fallen in love, or so she had thought. He had big plans of attending one of the "Big Ten" universities and hopefully from there, he would sign with a professional team. He had hoped that Joy would see that she was asking too much of him, too much for him to give up, but he would do what he could do.

Two years earlier, she had met Brad at a game when he moved to her small town of Alton. She was a member of the cheerleading squad. Brad had come in the middle of their sophomore year as his dad had moved their family after receiving a promotion with his company. Brad was a handsome young man with blond locks of hair tumbling down around his ears and falling into his eyes. His eyes were as blue as the ocean depths, and his smile was as captivating as if they were magnets—which, by the way, could hypnotically draw her to places she was normally afraid to go. He must have similarly thought of her, for it was during their first meeting that he asked her to go out with him. She said yes, only after playing fashionably hard to get. Something her mother had instilled in her. The attraction soon led to deep feelings that Joy had never experienced. She had had boyfriends before, but this was different.

She would often say to herself that he could be the one. But she was still not sure of that at first, or in the months that followed. However, as they continued to see only each other, the truth in her heart became more and more real that indeed he could be the one that she would spend her life with.

Brad and Joy had been dating for about a year. By their junior year in high school, Brad had become an all-star quarterback, and Joy was the absolute envy of all her friends. She worked hard in school and was a good student with a flair for writing and a desire to be a journalist someday. As most young girls in love do, she would spend hours fantasizing about how she and Brad and their career choices would help them to complement each other and bring about a blissful and never-ending marriage. She could see Brad scoring the big touchdowns and herself writing about them with glowing words that would make the world jealous of their true love. Their romance had blossomed into young love, first love—the kind grown-ups always assured her that, "You will just know when it happens."

Being the daughter of a deacon and coming from a respectable family, Joy and Brad had been successful in cooling down the heated passion that would unleash itself upon them as they stole away time from family and friends to be alone. As juniors in high school, they were excited to attend the prom. All the excitement and expectation hung over their imaginations as it was a given that they would go together and make their celebrity entrance into the high school gym that was made over to resemble a large ballroom. Joy had decided on her dress and Brad his tux. She had impatient thoughts as to what she and Brad would look like in their prom pictures. Joy envisioned herself holding a bouquet of flowers and Brad holding her. They would look like the all-American dream couple.

After months of anticipation and with nervous energy coursing through her body, the night finally came. She and Brad attended their prom with excitement enough to fill the air of the night. They danced, they talked with friends, they dined, and they danced some more. Brad, ever the star athlete, could not make the Fred Astaire moves as she had pictured him doing in her daydreams. He stepped on her feet a little too often, yet this had not disqualified them from becoming the envy of all eyes around them. If they had been seniors, without a doubt, they would have been crowned King and Queen of the prom.

During the night Brad had been sipping wine that he had secured from his brothers who were five years older than he. Joy had never succumbed to the wild callings of peer pressure as it related to alcohol. This was if truth be told, due to the stern warnings given by her father who produced an overwhelming fear in Joy. This night, however, she thought it would be safe to partake in just a little of the forbidden nectar. After all, they were becoming adults, and she had noticed that her mother would sneak a "snoot full" now and then. But she also noticed that it was only when her father would be out of town on business. Still no matter, she justified, I will not be home till late; Daddy will not find out.

As the night wore on, Brad and Joy found themselves alone. Brad had taken her to the back seat of his dad's car. The sense of liberty was swirling in the air. The night had been picture-perfect for both of them, not to mention the fact that the wine was beginning to cloud their resolve toward their normal restraint. Surprised by her own forwardness, it was Joy who pulled Brad in for a kiss that told Brad that she was his for tonight and forever. Thinking back to that night has often brought the two of them shame. It seemed strange to them how after that night, nothing was really the same for them. They knew that they had crossed a line that should not have been stepped over, but they were so intoxicated with a mixture of love and alcohol, that they were unable to see the line. Everything became blurred in their judgment and their self-control.

Months later, after the embarrassing confrontations with her parents and Brad, it was Joy who was feeling the burden of that night. She regretted her decision because the cost was far too great, not to mention lonely and painful. Neither Brad, her father, nor her mother had to expose their shame and body to near-perfect strangers like doctors and nurses. And each time, she could see in the faces of the medical staff the judgment that only unwed teenage mothers were worthy of receiving. To make everything worse and even more sinister, she was going against her own conscience. She wanted to do the right thing, and she examined, maybe for the first time in her life, the old adage that says, "Two wrongs do not make a right."

How, she wondered, could this "procedure" make right what had so terribly gone wrong in her life, her family, and with Brad and her? She knew, after having experienced the crossing of the earlier line, that she was about to cross another. This time the consequences were a question of life or death. She knew it was not just the death of her child in those dreadful consequences. For something had died in Joy as well. That night, she lost something she could never reclaim. It was the innocence that had covered her all through her young life. Now a veil had been lifted. She could see things in people, even in her own family, that she had never noticed before and would not have believed, even if it had been proven. They say you become a woman after the first time, but if this was being a woman, she longed already for the days of being Daddy's little girl draped in the innocence of almost total irresponsibility.

Even now, years later and in a deep sleep, these longings were just as real as they were then. They were more than a memory of past regrets that are usually chalked up to, "Live and learn." To Joy, they felt like an abyss in her very soul that could never be filled. No matter how full her life might become with things or memories, this emptiness, she believed, would always remain with her.

Drops of a light rain descended upon her unprotected cheek and forehead and gathered into small streams of water running down into her hair. She was startled by her sudden burst of alertness. It was early morning, and the sunrise was becoming more visible with bursting colors of light—orange, blue, and yellow. She had spent the night in a ditch beside the wrecked rental car. With her leg still in pain, but her body feeling the effects of a deep rest that had overtaken her, she was hurting and in need of help for the open cuts on her head and the possible fracture of her right ankle. She rolled over on the cold, wet earth beneath her. Then using a fallen tree limb for support, she managed to find a way to stand up. She still could not believe she had slept all night. She looked again at her cell phone hoping that a night of healing rest had somehow restored its ability to work again.

She also remembered her dream, the one that seemed to gain strength and increase in its agitation as she kept trying to shove it down. It was almost as if the dream itself were fighting its way up from the depths of the cave where she had hidden it. She felt that if that ever happened, she would be given over to the side of madness. So, once again she forced it back down and talked herself into taking care of the present matter of needing help and how she might get it.

In the distance she noticed smoke rising from somewhere in the woods. It seemed to her that it might be the smoke from a chimney. The thought of sitting in front of a warm fire right now would be heaven on earth. The night air and the light shower were starting to take effect on her now that she was finally awake and coming out of shock. For the first time since the wreck, she realized how very cold she was. Joy made the resolute decision that she would make her way to the warm fire instead of going up to the road and waiting for a car that might not come for hours in this little-traveled neck of the woods. She painfully picked up a stick to brace herself and started on her way to find the cozy fire and help. As she walked along the path, she wondered about her crew and what they must be thinking now that she was a full day late. She wondered how in the world they would ever find her out here. She began to regret taking the less-traveled route. She had thought that it would be good for her but was finding just the opposite to be true.

"Oh well," she spoke out loud, "I will just have to rely on what I learned as a young girl at wilderness camp. I might be a little rusty, but I do not plan on ending my life stranded in the woods and being dinner for a hungry, wild animal. I have come too far to give up now. Besides, this next story is going to be the one that puts my name at the top of the charts as far as reporting goes." So off she went on the next leg of this unexpected adventure.

CHAPTER THREE
The Crew

The previous day, Joy's crew arrived in Asheville at the hotel where they were all supposed to meet and begin the research and investigation of the story about the ring of perverted pastors. There were four crew members: Mat, the camera guy; Lucy, the records research guru; Ken, the runner and "gofer" guy; and Jay, the time and money manager of the group.

Mat, the camera guy, was the one who took the photos that they would use for proof when a story was ready to be printed. He had a great eye for knowing how to frame a subject in a way that could make them look even more sinister or more angelic than they really were in person. Joy heavily relied on this gift from her team member, for as it is said, "A picture is worth a thousand words." Mat's pictures were so compelling that even the least-interested reader would read the attached article to find out more. Mat was the quiet sort: you never really knew what he had on his mind or what he thought about anything that was being said by others. He seemed to always be looking for the next camera shot. He was so driven about his work, but he was really laid back and shy when it came to interacting with others. There was a standing joke within the group that Mat's best friend and wife were his camera. Therefore, the camera was lovingly named Cameron. It added to their banter that Cameron is also a Scottish name, which means "Crooked Nose." Therefore, Matt was married to a "woman" with an ugly crooked nose. They were so connected in their sarcastic wit. He did not seem to mind the joke at his expense; he was easy to get along with in that way. Nothing much upset him. However, when it came to the stories that they were discovering, Mat was very troubled and perplexed. As a matter of fact, he became quiet and reserved after a story. It was as if he needed to be alone to sort it all out and try to deal with the deep hurt in the faces of the people he had framed through the lens of his camera.

Then there was Lucy, the unyielding research guru. She was not afraid to talk to anyone. She used this gift of gab to get her into the long-lost files of almost every library—both public and private. She adored digging and was not satisfied until she had gotten to the root of a situation. But her digging didn't stop with records; she was notorious for trying to dig out those hidden secrets about people's lives as well. Almost no one's past was safe from Lucy's prying questions—no one's except Joy and her archived secrets. Even Lucy had been unable to crack Joy's secret Fort Knox vault-style code. For this reason, Joy avoided Lucy like the plague during the quiet and waiting times. Joy herself was not even sure of everything that lay deep within the caverns of her soul. She had pushed it down so many times that it was as deep as an old abandoned well. But this pushed Lucy toward insanity with curiosity. She chided Joy by prattling: "Release is good for the soul and **the truth** will set you free." One major rub for Joy—one that often ticked her off—was that Lucy accused her of believing deeply that "Truth would set you free" because Joy was dedicated to exposing people's pasts so they could stop their present behavior. This outraged Joy because she could not see how her secrets had anything to do with the types of secrets she had uncovered in others. Now Lucy was not a Christian, but her favorite catchphrase was: "In God's eyes, sin is sin." What that meant, Lucy really did not know, but she did understand that it had been a most helpful quote in getting people to open up to her. It somehow calmed their apprehensions and helped them to justify that their wrongs were no worse than anyone else's. Nonetheless, Joy and Lucy worked well together, but only because Lucy was the best at digging up the research, not because Lucy was Joy's personal friend.

Number three in the group but number one to everyone as far as being their favorite team player, was Ken, the "gofer" guy. He was the one who went for anything that everyone needed. He loved serving his teammates. He would go for coffee, meals, film—really anything that anyone needed or even wanted for that fact. He was a very generous soul, and he liked to surprise team members by picking up some of their favorite things even when they did not ask him to. For example, Lucy loved jellybeans, Mat loved nuts, Jay was a lover of car magazines, and Joy was an avid collector of porcelain dolls. Ken would buy a doll whenever she could find one that was truly different and unique. He would buy all these things at his own expense because he loved the expressions on their faces when he brought them unexpected treats. Ken lightened the mood of the group when they were dealing with a particularly disturbing case. Joy was not the only one that genuinely liked Ken; everyone else enjoyed his presence. He made them feel special and cemented the group into more of a team.

Ken spent a lot of time and energy on finding beautiful and one-of-a-kind dolls for Joy because he secretly had a crush on her. He thought she was pretty and smart, but Joy never noticed. She was always so afraid that she might have to share the secrets in her own heart, that she tended not to see the need to get to know anyone else well enough to discover what made their heart beat a little faster. But he was such a nice guy who did not care that she didn't respond in kind. He enjoyed being allowed to please her in some small way.

Last was Jay, the time and money manager of the group. He was very tightly laced because his job required that he make sure that the team came in under budget. This type of crew, which had to travel out of town for extended stays, definitely needed a budget policeman, and Jay was up for the challenge. Nothing was done that was not approved by Jay. He was tight with money, and he made reservations for the group at less-than-desirable hotels. Very rarely, if ever, would he allow the group to put a very expensive dinner on the tab. He believed that if they wanted to splurge above the allotted budget, they needed to make up the difference out of their own pockets. Most of the time, dinner was takeout in one of the hotel rooms while they collaborated on a lead or watched a goofy movie on cable to relax. They often gave Jay a hard time, but they knew he was really helping them in the long run. His firm ways usually kept them under budget for the year, and this translated into cold, hard cash for the team in the form of very healthy bonuses. Besides, since they were about the business of helping others, it would not be desirable for their faces to be on the front page of another paper showing them drunk or in a compromising situation. Such behavior might cause them to be disqualified as credible journalists. Besides, none of them had families at home, so they were glad to spend time with each other like a regular family. Even though they would tell Jay, from time to time, that he could divide a penny ten different ways, they still liked him as a team member and a friend.

Despite their obvious differences, they were a close-knit group, and they were beginning to be concerned for Joy and where she might be. They called her cell phone and left message after message. She had been known to be late on several occasions recently, but she had not been this late before. Even so, they knew how strong-willed and independent Joy was. They were not so worried as to stop everything and go find her. They thought that she might be chasing another lead and would call them soon. Therefore, they put their heads together to come up with a plan of action to find Joy and continue following up on the story that they had come to uncover. After a short meeting, it was decided that Mat and Lucy would chase the story lead, and Ken and Jay would try to find Joy. They all agreed to this plan and started off in their separate directions.

Mat and Lucy began by first trying to find the pastors so that they could follow them and maybe catch them on film early in the game. This would help them determine the next step to take. They carefully looked through the file. According to the records, the pastors all worked one day a week at a soup kitchen, another day a week at an orphanage, and another third at the local daycare. Of course, this is how it was thought that they were able to get away with the molestations since they had gotten to know the victims before they even became victims. If this were true, then the evil within these men's hearts would even be a greater evil than first thought, because this would prove premeditation. That is, they would be doing good for children only to have the opportunity to do them great harm later. This type of abuse had been seen among most child predators, but this appeared to be a group of predators who were standing together at every step. Therefore, Lucy and Mat felt that this case would take a great deal of coordination and planning among the members and that the men would be bound to slip up sooner or later. But the sooner, the better both Lucy and Mat agreed. These men had to be stopped as soon as possible. So they set off for the orphanage to interview some people and see what they could uncover.

It did not take long before they were at the Little Lost Lambs orphanage. They pulled up front and saw about ten children playing outside on a jungle gym. They both thought about which of these children had been hurt and how truly sad it was that they had lost their families—and then for someone to take their innocence too. Suddenly, Lucy and Mat became silent for a moment at the thought of it all. They watched the children as if they longed for the day to play again and be able to laugh truly and deeply.

Mat said to Lucy, "You know, if these children have been hurt, they sure are resilient. Watch how they play . . . as if they do not have a problem in the world. I really wish I could lay my burdens down like that."

Lucy sighed dreamily and said, "Yeah, that would be great."

Mat pulled out his camera, got out of the car, and went over to take a few pictures of the children as they enjoyed their playtime. It felt good to be able to take some pictures of happy faces for a change.

Then a worker approached Mat and Lucy and asked, "Can I help you?"

Lucy told her that they were with a newspaper and that they were doing a story on a group of pastors who worked together at some of the local charities every week. Of course, the real reason for their visit did not need to be told at this time; Mat and Lucy were looking for leads.

The worker gleefully smiled and said, "Oh, you must be talking about the Fabulous Four. They would never own that title as they are all too modest to refer to themselves in that way, but that is what we call them. Come on in, and I will tell you about these wonderful men."

She showed Mat and Lucy to the den where they could all be seated comfortably. She then asked, "Would either of you like something cold to drink?"

Lucy and Mat shook their heads to indicate no as they sat down.

The orphanage worker continued by saying, "Now, about these men of God. They come here every week and do whatever needs to be done. One time, all the children had the stomach virus, and so did I. Those four saints came in and cleaned up after all the children and were able to get small amounts of soup into the kids' stomachs so the children could start to feel better. That day, I saw a lot of miracles, not just one or two. Knowing they were here helping the children was healing to my body as well."

Mat looked curiously at Lucy. Lucy seemed just as puzzled but a little more skeptical because she could see how this would have made the children a prime target for the sickness of these men. The children were weak, and the main caregiver and protector were also out of the way.

Mat had to ask the obvious question, "Were you not worried about leaving these precious children with these strange men?"

The worker shouted at Mat with great anger, "Exactly what do you mean by the term *strange men*?" You could tell that she had obviously been offended.

"How could you even ask such a question?" the caregiver chided. "I have given my very life to these children. They were hurt before they were brought here, and I vow to every child, that once they are here, they are safe. I tell every one of them the story of how Jesus, the shepherd, had one hundred sheep, and one was lost, and the lost one was so valuable to him that he left the ninety-nine for a time to go and find the one little, lost lamb. That is how we got our name. Here they feel and know how very valuable and important they are to Jesus, me, and the other staff. Those four preachers give tirelessly and unselfishly to all of us." With great passion in her voice, she said clearly and distinctly: "Do you think for one minute that I would ever let anyone in here that would hurt my children or even think of such things? I think it is time for you to go now! I will show you to the door." After abruptly standing up, she escorted them to the door and gathered the children around her like a mother hen who was protecting them. Then she said, "Goodbye, and I hope that you will both find someone as wonderful as these four preachers to help you in your time of need."

Mat and Lucy were amazed at the amount of respect that these men had acquired from the caregiver. They wondered how she could not have seen at least one red flag in all these years; how she could have been so blind, they thought. But they also thought that she protested the questions a little too much and feared that she might be hiding something as well.

Lucy, ever the digger, thought out loud, "Maybe she was afraid of losing her job or her standing in the community. Or worse yet, what if she is secretly in the center of the ring with the preachers? What if she gets some of the profits from the pictures they take?"

Whatever was going on, this encounter drove them to try to find out all they could about these preachers, what they might be up to, and who might be involved with them in these crimes against the innocent little ones of this town.

Next, they arrived at the Soul Harvest soup kitchen as they were starting to serve the noonday meal. Mat and Joy were amazed to see how many people and children needed food and some spiritual comfort. Neither Mat nor Lucy had witnessed an operation of this sort close up. At that moment, Mat began to be drawn away by the faces he saw. He lost track of his bearing and began snapping pictures. He felt as if he were in a post-traumatic situation following some catastrophe such as a flood or tornado; the people looked so tired, shocked, and dirty. Mat was puzzled why there were so many; so he stopped a worker and asked her.

Shelly was her name. She was kind with bright eyes and a happy face that seemed to come from deeper than just her smile—more like deep peace. This really intrigued Mat, and he asked to take her picture. She said, "Okay . . . I guess" with a curious look as to why this stranger wanted her picture.

Mat had seen so much sadness, and to see this peace was something he felt like he needed to capture to help him make it through those times of "sorting it all out." But after the picture was taken, she went on to tell him that a very large snowstorm of blizzard proportions was coming down from the mountains. "These people made it out in time to get to the city and to the shelter." She further explained, "Because it was an unexpected blizzard and out of the normal snow season, everyone was unprepared. They were told to get out because they would be trapped if they stayed, and the snow would be so deep and heavy that their roofs might not stand the weight, and the temperatures were going to keep the snowfall around so long that the food supply might run out." With nervousness in her voice, she said, "So much for global warming, huh? So that is why they are all here and dirty. Many of them began in cars like you, but then the cars became stuck in the snow, and they had to walk to the nearest town for help in getting here. We will not know for a while who did not make it off that mountain. The police and rescue workers are all out in full force trying to rescue as many as they can before the storm starts again. It has stalled for now."

Mat said, "I noticed it was a little colder than I expected. But a blizzard of this magnitude? How is this possible this time of year?"

Shelly nodded politely and said, "God is the only one who knows the answer to that question. And I have learned that even in the bad things, God has a good reason. I keep on praying and working here to help whoever I can. Sometimes bad things happen in this world—some by our own hands and some by the hands of others, but God can use all of them to bring us to the end of ourselves."

Mat stood there in shock that she could look so happy and believe so deeply. He secretly wished he could be like Shelly. He became lost in his thoughts for a moment.

"Mr. . . . Mr.?" Shelly said as she tugged at his sleeve in hopes of arousing him out of his daydream. "Are you going to help? Or are you going to stand there and look like a blizzard victim yourself?" Shelly softly chided.

Mat at once remembered that Joy was out there somewhere. He said, "Shelly, how long do we have until this storm reaches us, and will it be as bad as they expect?"

Shelly said, "We are being told that we only have twenty-four hours to get ready and that it will be a big one. But outside of that, we do not know anything more."

Mat thanked Shelly and quickly ran to find Lucy who by this time had been drafted to read a story to some of the waiting children.

"Lucy," Mat blurted out, "there is a blizzard coming in twenty-four hours, and we still do not know where Joy is. Let's go and find Ken and Jay and tell them to call the police, the airport, and the car rental company to see if they can locate her!"

But Lucy looked at the children and did not have the heart to leave them unattended; she could tell they were still in some sort of shock. Mat sensed this and knew that he could be more help here than out on the road looking for Joy. Mat said, "I'll take over here. These people need help too but hurry. You drive better and faster than I do, and you are better at rallying people to help you than I am."

So, Lucy quickly agreed and grabbed her coat as she ran out the door. She tried to catch Ken and Jay on their cell phone, but she got a busy signal; she left a message for them to call her right back.

CHAPTER FOUR
The Fabulous Four?

Ring, ring... ring, ring. Lucy picked up the phone and said, "Hello." Ken's friendly voice was on the phone. He asked, "What's up, Luus?"

Lucy, still breathing heavily from all the excitement, asked Ken if he had heard from Joy.

He said, "No, not yet; we were just about to call the car rental company and see what they knew. We thought maybe she had mentioned to someone what route she was going to take. Where is Mat? Did you guys get any good pictures?"

Lucy, frustrated by the chitchat from Ken like nothing was wrong, began to speak very firmly to Ken, "Look, we do not have time to talk about the story right now. I just left Mat at a soup kitchen with a bunch of people who were relocated from their homes because of a major blizzard that is headed straight for us. We have less than twenty-four hours to find Joy and get back to Mat at the kitchen before this thing hits us!"

Ken, whose temperament was mostly slow and easygoing, found it hard to believe that there was a blizzard coming. He dismissively laughed as he poked back at Lucy, "Oh Luus, you are big kidder. What kind of trick are you and Mat up to this time?"

"Ken!" Lucy fired back, "this is not a joke; now tell me where we can meet, and I will tell you the plan."

Ken became very alarmed at Lucy's sense of urgency and told her that they could meet at the hotel because he and Jay were going there to see if Joy had shown up. Lucy was relieved that Ken finally believed her, so they made a plan that they would meet at the hotel parking lot in ten minutes.

Ken and Jay arrived at the hotel parking lot at about the same time as Lucy. She jumped out of the car and ran over to meet them.

Jay, seeing Lucy's obvious panic, which was not at all like her, questioned, "What's up girl?"

She was almost in tears to the point of hysteria. She began to tell her friends about leaving to find Joy—and fast. She explained to them about the storm coming and how little time they had.

Jay, ever the time manager immediately began to mentally align everything that they needed to do. He said, "Don't worry, my parents live up where there is a lot of snow, so I have snow chains and know how to put them on. I also have emergency supplies in case we get stuck. We are going to have to go to the airport and try to trace her steps from there. Ken and I have had no luck here in town. No one at the hotel has seen or heard from her either." Quickly and with determination, Jay got the trunk of his car open and started inspecting his tire chains and checking out his emergency equipment. He figured that it took about two hours to get to the Charlotte Airport and that they should be able to trace her steps from there. Jay said calmly, "Surely, we can make that trip and back and find Joy in less than twenty-four hours. We will be fine. Don't panic, Lucy."

Lucy quickly stated, "Jay, you do not know what we saw at that soup kitchen. These people lived on that mountain, and they have dealt with snow all their lives, but they were totally in shock. They were hungry, dirty, and cold and did not know what to do next, and there were so many of them. They all said that they had never seen a storm like this in their entire lives. One man was one hundred and four years old. So don't tell me to take it easy. This is not a time for calm."

Jay, trying to help Lucy get a grip on reality, just nodded his head and said, "We will leave right now, and we will find her."

Lucy found herself partially relieved that Jay was in charge, so she got in the back seat of the car and buckled up. They stopped at a local store on the way out of town and got a map and asked the teller for the quickest route to Charlotte.

The teller pointed toward the most direct route while he rang up the map, but then added, "You *do* know that there is a blizzard coming, right?"

Jay assured him that they were aware of it but that they needed to find a friend before the storm got there. The clerk looked concerned and wished them safety and good luck.

Just then a customer in the store tapped Jay on the shoulder and said, "I am sorry that I overheard your conversation. But if you don't mind, can I have prayer with you before you leave so that God will help keep all of you safe and help your friend too?"

Jay, Ken, and Lucy were shocked but willing to try anything, so they said, "Sure."

The stranger led everyone in the store to all hold hands while he prayed for them. He prayed like no one they had ever heard before. They could feel someone else's presence in the store that had not been there previously.

Then the man began to pray for their friend saying, "Oh, Lord we also pray for Joy and that you will watch over her in this time of trial and keep her safe in your loving arms. Help her to see your truth and your face and know that she is truly loved and cared for. Amen."

As soon as Lucy, Ken, and Jay opened their eyes to say thank you to the stranger, they noticed he was gone. Lucy asked the clerk, "Where did that man go? We wanted to thank him."

The clerk said, "Oh, that is just the way he and his three preacher friends are. They will bless your heart but never stay around to be thanked. They believe that the praise should go to their God, but not to them."

Just then Lucy's jaw dropped, "Do you mean one of the Fabulous Four?"

"Yeah, some people call them that around here, but I am surprised that out-of-town folks like yourselves would know them by that title."

Jay asked Lucy what she was talking about. She told him to get in the car and that she would explain on the way. After she told them the story that she and Mat had heard at the orphanage and what had happened, Jay and Ken were shocked that one of these men had just prayed for them.

Ken sarcastically blurted out the obvious, "Boy, what an irony we have here. We come here in hopes of exposing these men, and one of them ends up praying for Joy and us. Wait a minute! Did any of you tell the preacher that our friend's name was Joy?"

Both shook their heads no, but they were curious as to why Ken wanted to know.

"In his prayer, he prayed for our friend, Joy. How did he know that her name was Joy? What if he knows her name because they have her hidden to keep her from talking? She could be in danger. We must involve the police."

"Do you think these men are after us too?" Lucy chimed in.

Ken, ever the cautious one, said, "We might need to be careful about who we speak to."

Lucy then remembered, "What about Mat?" The file we had on these men stated that they go to that same soup kitchen. What if these preachers get there and figure out who Mat is?"

They decided to call Mat and tell him to only listen and keep his eyes open, but not to tell anyone why he was actually there. Ken, Lucy, and Jay would go to the police and see what they could find out.

"Mat, this is Jay. I want to you listen to me, but try not to talk loud enough for anyone else to hear you, okay?"

Mat says calmly, "Sure, I hear you."

Jay went on to tell Mat the situation. "We were on our way to Charlotte to pick up Joy's trail. However, when we stopped in a local store to get a map, one of those four men that you and Lucy heard about was there. He asked to pray for us and our friend. But Mat, here is the kicker. We never told him that our friend's name was Joy, but he mentioned her name in his prayer. We are going to the police because we think he knew her name. After all, they have her. We are afraid that they might come to the soup kitchen and try to get you next."

Mat interrupted Jay and spoke as in a special code so no one in the soup kitchen could catch on, "Yeah, hum . . . that will work, the four "packages" have already arrived and are right here beside me. But for the other plan you mentioned, you might have some problems finding help. The help you will need is up the mountain bringing down more people. And from what I am seeing, you might be wrong ab…" Just then, the phone went dead.

Jay had really become alarmed by this time and feared that they might all be in trouble.

Hanging up the phone slowly, Jay informed the others: "Mat said that they were right there beside him, and he said that the police are tied up helping people off the mountain; then the phone went dead when he was about to tell me that I was wrong about something. We need to get back to the soup kitchen and see if we can help Mat. I will call the paper and let them know the situation and see if they can get the Charlotte police involved in finding Joy." Lucy and Ken became very afraid for themselves and their friends, but they knew Jay was right and they needed to get to Mat as soon as possible.

Ken, Jay, and Lucy arrived at the soup kitchen about a half hour later. They were afraid and exhausted and wanted to find Mat as soon as possible and get back to the hotel. By the time they arrived, the rescue workers had brought in even more people. The makeshift shelter was so crowded that they could not see anything—especially just one man. They started asking questions of those that would talk with them. Everyone they asked remembered Mat as the fellow that was taking pictures and helping the children to feel better by letting them take some pictures as well. But no one they talked to knew where he was.

Then they ran into Shelly. Not knowing that she and Mat had been talking a lot, Jay asked her if she knew where Mat was.

Shelly said with a smile, "Yeah, he left a little while ago with the four preachers that help us out every week."

Jay replied quickly with a sense of urgency in his voice, "Shelly, where did they go?"

Shelly answered, "Oh, they said something about getting Mat to help them take some pictures of the children that had been brought in by the police. There is so much commotion with the coming storm that some parents and their kids are getting separated."

Jay said to Shelly, "Thanks," and then turned to leave.

But Shelly stopped him and said, "You had better stay here. They just said that the storm is moving faster than expected, and you will only get trapped. We really need some extra hands here."

But Jay was determined to find Mat. He told Shelly, "Thanks, but we will have to risk it." Not knowing what to expect or the danger ahead, the three of them headed for the car. But just then the storm hit, and they could not see their hands in front of their faces, much less drive the car. They now had no choice but to stay. This was the worst feeling of helplessness that any of them had ever felt in their lives.

Shelly saw them come back in and jokingly said, "Some people never listen. Well, come on; you must be hungry, and you will need your energy. This is going to be a long night."

CHAPTER FIVE
Safe?

Scars . . . so many scars . . . they appeared to be hideous reminders of the deep wounds of his past. They were marks that repulsed her, but at the same time, they drew out the curiosity of the reporter entrenched within her.

She stopped to question herself; should I approach him? I wonder if he is safe. Immediately, she began to hear the recorded message of her mother's voice that always played in her mind like a never-ending dripping faucet. She could even hear the words in her mother's condemning voice, "All men are evil and will hurt you. Just look at what your father has done to us."

Yet she was truly in need of rescue, and this stranger seemed to be her only available option. She stood quiet and still to observe him as he chopped wood.

His arms were tan and strong, and he hit each piece of wood as if he had frustration that needed to be released.

She thought to herself, "Why would he be way out here in the middle of nowhere? Does he have a family? Where does he work?" So many fears but also so many questions. For the first time in a long time, she was unsure of her next move.

Just then he turned sharply and looked in her direction. He acted like a mountain tracker who was able to hear her breathe. When he turned to look at her, she saw his face. She gasped in horror. For at that moment, she saw that his face was as covered with deep scars as his back. She searched her mind to try to determine what terrible lot had befallen this man to produce such horrible scars.

Yet in his eyes, in his deep blue, sad eyes, there seemed to be longing and hurting that leapt up from his very soul to capture her. At that moment, she felt less like a timid rabbit and more like a lost kitten looking for a home to belong to. Something about his eyes spoke to her and moved her to believe that he needed to help her as much as she needed to be helped.

"Who's there?" he shouted while reaching for his shirt to cover the scars that plagued his body. It was as if he was suddenly very aware that his appearance would repulse another human being.

Shyly, she took a deep breath and slowly stood up from the brush where she was hiding, she said with a tremble in her voice, "My name is . . . Joy."

"What are you doing here?" he said firmly but also with a hint of curiosity mixed with suspicion.

"I need help!" Joy almost cried. He began to move in her direction buttoning up his shirt and putting on his cap.

Joy stood still awaiting his approach. She knew there was no sense in trying to maintain an "in-control" appearance and attitude. It was as if two members of a feuding family had just happened to meet, not knowing what to expect from the other.

As he came closer to Joy, he noticed she was favoring her right leg, her ankle to be exact. "What happened to you?" he asked.

"I was in an accident. I am a reporter, and I am already a day late. I was supposed to meet my crew in Asheville yesterday. I ran off the road a few miles back and slept in the ditch all last night. I may have sprained my ankle, but I don't think it is broken."

"Okay, okay," he said sharply, letting her know from his tone that she had more than answered his questions. "So, you were in an accident," he said.

"Yes, I just told you that," Joy answered back realizing she had begun to speed talk. She always talked too fast and gave out a lot of frivolous information when she was nervous. She hated the quiet lulls in a conversation. Something about those pauses scared her.

Suddenly, he bent down to get a closer look at her ankle. He looked up at her for a quick glance into her face, waiting for approval before he inspected further. Sensing her apprehensiveness but also her need for help, he reached out with his hands and rolled up her pant leg, just enough so he could get her shoe off.

Joy noticed how gentle his hands were to the touch of her ankle as he took a closer look. His hands were rough like sandpaper but gentle and kind to her injury. As he continued to check her ankle, she winced in pain as he began to prod it for the seriousness of the injury. As Joy began to feel the pain that shot up from her ankle to the rest of her body, she became faint. The pain was more than she could handle, so she found herself falling toward the ground as her eyes rolled back into her head.

But as quick as a mountain lion, he rose up and took hold of Joy before she had the chance to fall too far.

Joy had passed out from the journey, the pain, and the hunger, so he picked her up and took her into his strong but gentle arms. He noticed the cuts on the top of her head. It appeared that the rain had washed away the blood that had been matted in her hair, but the jacket she was wearing was covered with blood. It was then that he began to understand that she was hurt worse than he had first thought. Forgetting everything else for the moment, he walked up the steps of the back porch of his small but cozy cabin. With his left hand still securing the fragile body of a woman he knew nothing about except that her name was Joy and that she was hurt, he opened the screen door and walked across the threshold of his humble home.

Carrying her into the den, he placed her limp body on the sofa and went into the room adjacent to the kitchen to get another pillow and some blankets. As he entered the den again, he found Joy in a deep, weary sleep. So, he quietly unfolded the blanket and placed it over her, and then cradling the back of her head in his hand, he gently lifted her head up just enough to wedge a feathery soft pillow between the armrest of the couch and her head. As he checked the blankets and assured himself that Joy was warm enough, he put the back of his right hand upon Joy's forehead and checked for any symptoms of a fever. It was obvious to him that this woman needed help. He noted that she had put on such an air of invincibility and independence that he just knew she would not allow anyone to take care of her if she could absolutely help it.

Wwhhrrrrr . . . the teapot began to whistle loudly as Joy started to open her eyes. Looking around for anything familiar that would remind her of where she was, she at first felt a quick burst of panic and sat up on the sofa abruptly forgetting her ankle. She twisted it in the blankets and once again the pain brought everything back. Removing the covers from around her feet, she noticed her ankle had been wrapped in an athletic bandage, and the cuts on her head had been dressed also with some layers of gauze. She could hear him in the kitchen as he removed the teapot from the wood-burning stove, which immediately silenced the small cabin once again.

Joy grabbed the armrest of the couch with both hands trying to find the physical strength as well as the balance that would allow her to stand up and move into the kitchen.

Just as she was lifting herself up ever so slowly from the couch, she heard his quick, snapping voice insisting, "No, no, no!" He continued to gently scold her, "You need to stay off your feet. You are hurt worse than you think."

His voice came as such a surprise that she forgot that she wanted to stand and slumped back down onto the sofa.

He said, "Stay there and I will bring you something to eat and drink." He left her sight only for a moment as he went back into the kitchen and picked up a tray that held a bowl of soup, a cup of hot tea, a glass of water, and the needed silverware and napkins. After he brought the tray into the den, he nudged a footstool from across the floor with his foot. He pushed it until it rested in front of Joy's feet.

He placed the tray down and said, "You must be hungry and thirsty, so I made you some soup and tea." After a brief silence that seemed to carry an echo, he said, "It's not broken."

Joy, looking a little puzzled and still not sure of this stranger who had taken her in and bandaged her wounds, asked, "What?"

"Your ankle. . . it's not broken," he said.

"Oh," Joy replied, "yes, thank you." Joy could smell the aroma of the hot soup and the tea that waited to appease her roaring hunger. She took the spoon and with her free hand, she carefully pulled the soup up to the edge of the tray and began submerging the spoon in the hot broth. As she took her time, she was allowing her nose to tell her to reject or accept the meal that lay before her because she was still leery of this stranger with all the scars. As the smell communicated that this was what she needed, her mouth quivered with anticipation of filling her hunger. The soup was very good. Immediately she placed the spoon down and grabbed for the water, turning it up as fast as she could gulp it down. Streams of water ran down the sides of her mouth as she consumed the entire glass. Slamming the empty glass back down on the tray, she once again took up where she left off with the bowl of soup. She was alarmed by how her hunger had reduced her table manners to those of a wild animal. Looking around the small space, she noticed over the fireplace hearth a picture of an angel watching over two children as they crossed an old rickety bridge. Then her eyes fell on a small stack of books beside what must have been his sitting chair. Then she noticed one of the books. It looked like a worn-out old Bible.

"Oh good, I am stuck with a religious nut with no one to rescue me," she mumbled to herself.

Hoping he had not seen her grimace at the summary of her inspection, she asked, "What time is it, and can I use your phone?"

At this, he responded, "It is evening, probably about five or six, and I have no phone for you to use."

If Joy had been with her crew, she would have made some wisecrack about the music in the movie *Deliverance*, but his answer only made her anxious. "What do you mean it is five or six? Don't you know the exact time? What about a clock or a watch?

The scarred man answered, "I have a radio, but that is about it."

"How long have I been resting?" Joy asked, though somewhat taken aback by his answer regarding the time.

"You were out about six hours; you must have had some night in these woods. I find it pretty remarkable that you made it this far," he added.

At this point, Joy blurted out with amazement at her own words, "You're not going to hurt me, are you?"

"Why, do I look like I'm going to hurt you?" he asked as if playing the devil's advocate.

Joy had no sooner heard his answer than she began to feel a deep sense of embarrassment instead of feeling afraid. With her face flushed a deep red, she moved right into her next question realizing she did not know his name. Without ever apologizing for her insulting comment, she asked, "So, what's your name?" Joy could not bring herself to investigate his face any longer for fear he might see in her eyes what she was thinking.

"Caleb Nobah is my first and middle name, but my enemies call me Scarback, and I have no friends to speak of, so you can call me whatever you like."

Joy could tell that he was not willing to give information without being prodded to do so, but she was intrigued by the name and wondered if it meant anything in particular. So, she asked, "What does your name mean?"

Silence filled the air. She knew he would not answer that question regardless of how many times she would ask.

"Listen," she said, hoping to change tactics, "I need to get help. Can you take me somewhere so I can use a phone or get to a hospital?"

At this, he got up and walked over to the coffee table beside his sitting chair and turned on the radio. He dialed through the static until a voice could be heard clear enough to make out what was being said. Joy heard the radio jock sounding a note of alarm to all his listeners.

"Heavy snow. Blizzard status. I repeat: this system is expected to bring heavy snow through North Carolina. It will be mixed with ice and sleet for the next twenty-four to thirty-six hours. This will be a fast-approaching storm, so unless it is absolutely necessary, the highway patrol says to stay off the roads. If you have an emergency, you should dial 911 for help. This has been a weather bulletin from WAGL, the place to turn for . . ." Click.

Caleb had turned off the radio, hoping Joy had gotten the real message. He knew she needed to be reassured of his intentions, but he had to make sure she understood that he was not keeping her there against her will. There was just no way to get help right now. In fact, he really didn't want her there any more than she wanted to be there, but a sense of duty to help someone like Joy pushed him on.

"So that's it!" Joy exclaimed. Joy began to yell and become very sarcastic, "No phones, no help, a storm—no, no, correction—a blizzard is coming with ice and sleet for good measure, and not even a television in sight, and you, the poster child for Hermits R Us! This is just like God to do this to me. Great, just great!" Joy always felt God was out to get her, somehow.

She had this twisted view of how God intervened in her life, and "this was just like Him," she thought to herself. At times, she had come to see her life as a never-ending battle with God. She continued to lose herself in her thoughts. She was convinced that He would allow her only enough success, fun, and pleasure to keep her chasing after the proverbial dangling carrot, but never afford her the privilege of catching the carrot. This was just one of the paradoxes concerning God and his motives that she had rehearsed in her mind over and over. But she could also see a paradox in the small everyday things as well as the big events of her life; where she was now and what she was experiencing would most definitely qualify as a big event. She had a knack for blaming God for not allowing her to ever find a decent parking space as well as giving God credit for every clumsy act she ever committed. She held God personally responsible for dropping things like grocery bags, but she would never admit that it might just have something to do with trying to carry too much at one time.

And she often had displays of anger resulting in confrontations with inanimate objects if they did not work the way she wanted them to. Her mind began to wander back to the times her crew would just stand back and watch when she would have those one-sided spats. At those moments they found her quite entertaining. She remembered that they once caught her in the kitchen of the hotel suite trying to make coffee with an old and unreliable machine. It was early morning, and she was the only one awake, but Joy needed her coffee to get going.

Everyone in the suite was jolted out of their beds by the sound of Joy standing in the kitchen screaming at the uncooperative pot, "Do you want a piece of me? I am in no mood for this foolishness; now give me my coffee!"

Just then, everyone heard one perk and then two and suddenly there was coffee. Joy's tantrums usually did not produce such success, but still, this was a quirky part of her that the others said they loved to see. Joy wanted to believe that there was a big plan or some cosmic purpose to the bad things that happened to people, but sometimes, she just could not understand why so much of that bad energy found its way to her doorstep.

Just then, it dawned on her that she was being rude to her host: first, she had insulted him, and now she was daydreaming and totally ignoring him. "I am sorry," she mustered up more out of a realization that she did not want to be thrown out with a blizzard on the way. "I don't know where all that came from, you know . . . about you being a hermit and all. I really am sorry." Wow, Joy thought, finding the courage to say, "I am sorry," is usually impossible for me. She began to mentally pat herself on the back and thought, "You go, girl."

He told her, "You'll have to stay here until the storm passes, and there is no other option."

Joy thought about suggesting that if they would leave now, surely, they could beat the storm. Or maybe she could just walk out as she had walked in, but then she realized darkness was fast approaching, and this cabin had been hard enough to find in the light of day. Joy began to rethink the path that led her to this cabin. She had walked with the help of a stick for about two miles.

Then she remembered that to the left of the road, there was a trail that opened onto a kind of driveway on the side of a hill. After going about two hundred yards up and over the hill, she spotted the small cabin in the cove. She remembered that there were several junk cars out to the side of the yard and an old Ford truck. But replaying the journey that led her to the cabin only helped her to realize that she was not going to be able to go anywhere until this storm was over. She would have to rely on the kindness of this stranger if she was going to get anywhere. But even though she did not want to say or be obvious, the scars on his face were alarming to her. She tried to make sure that he did not catch her looking directly at his marks. She did not want to embarrass him. After all, he had been very nice so far. But she was always distrustful of everyone.

With a sigh of defeat, Joy blurted out unkindly: "I have to admit that I do not like this situation in which I find myself. I find it extremely nerve-wracking, and you do not look like the sort . . ." She caught herself and thought better of her next words. She was on his territory with no control and about to insult the only help she has seen so far. It was as if Caleb pretended to not hear a single word of insult that Joy had lashed out at him. She was still revved up, but she had caught herself and stopped before she said anything about the scars. She felt extremely self-conscious around him already. If she tried to talk to him, she feared that he would notice her staring at his scars.

There were repeated marks of flesh once torn and ripped from some form of violent encounter. Whether an accident or intentional, Joy could not tell, and neither was he telling. It did appear to Joy that whatever had inflicted these marks had been very evil.

Caleb was the first to break the silence. He told Joy, matter-of-factly, that she could sack out on the couch or in another room off the back porch.

Joy wanted to put as much distance between herself and his room as possible, so she took the back porch room for herself.

After making sure she had plenty of blankets and encouraging Joy to make herself at home, he closed her bedroom door behind him as he left her alone for the night. With the door closed behind him and his hand still on the doorknob, he felt a worrisome thought quickly dash through his head: "What are you doing this for?" He really liked being alone; it was peaceful for him to not have to see the fear in people's eyes as they noticed his disfigurement. He let go of the doorknob and crept toward his own room, which was on the front side of the cabin.

Joy had sensed his presence standing outside her door for just a moment too long, and she released the pent-up oxygen in her lungs as she heard him walk away. She turned off the lamp on the nightstand beside her bed, laid back on the flannel sheets that warmed quickly to her touch, and covered herself with two multicolored handmade quilts.

Entering his personal domain, Caleb would forgo his nightly ritual of reading a few chapters in the book that once had been collecting dust on his grandfather's handmade bookshelf. He loved to read, and he would order new books that caught his interest. But his weakness was that he would lovingly display them on a shelf and make a promise to read them one day soon. He would eventually get to them, but he seemed to always be two or three dozen books behind. A variety of topics interested him: carpentry, automobiles, detective stories, and spy stories. But books about faith and how God intervened in the lives of real people were the ones that piqued his interest the most. He started off his mornings by reading a few chapters from his worn-out Bible that was faithfully stationed by his favorite chair. Usually, this time was accompanied by a strong cup of coffee and a silence that he had grown rather accustomed to.

But regrettably, he knew that this ritual would not be possible for at least the next few days while he had company to attend to. He could tell that Joy's disposition would only make him the source of greater ridicule. Therefore, to keep the peace, he decided that he would either study at bedtime or get up before Joy arose. He felt that her position about the way he lived would grow exhausting to him after a few days of being locked up in the cabin due to the storm. Not only was she someone who judged people harshly, but she also seemed to be very distrustful of him even though he had only tried to help her. He had lived through more than his share of winter storms, but this one was really causing alarm. He could tell by the radio reports that this was going to be out of the ordinary, to say the least. He knew that the ordeal would not be over in just a day or two even though Joy was counting on that.

He began to worry about Joy getting the fever, cabin fever, that is. He recognized that he might be hard-pressed to calm her down. She had only been here for a few hours and had already lost it and purposely cut him with that double-edged sword called a tongue. Her words made him think of the scars he bore. Her words also made him realize that even though she would dare not admit it, she was really scared. That is why she ranted at him earlier. He knew something about being afraid too. As he got into bed, he prayed that God would help him to help her.

At first, sleep would not come. But later in the night, he dozed off to the flashing images that often invaded his mind in his slumber. These images caused his body to feel as if he had physically gone back in time. The torturous sounds and the cries haunted him. He felt trapped—like he would never be free.

CHAPTER SIX
Letters

He could see her face filled with fear. The images, once again, were so real that it was as if he were reliving the past in the present. Tears streamed down her face as open sobs and cries pitched forth from her mouth. Her small and timid hands tried to cover herself as they shook with desperation for what she knew was coming. The sound of leather cracking down on her small and weak body was more than he could suffer. Without ever thinking about his own fears or the pain he would have to endure, which was always greater than hers, he broke free from his mother's grip and ran to his sister, and pushed her down on the floor, sacrificing his own flesh for the protection of hers.

There were sounds of crying from the others in the room, screaming, "Stop it, Daddy. Stop it; you are killing him!"

He could still hear the leather cracking as it came down on his back. Somehow at this moment, he did not feel as much pain as he did when he had to stand and watch her being hit repeatedly at the hands of this wicked man they called father. This was only one of such beatings that he endured for her sake.

Another day began to play in his mind, but this time he was running with his little sister's hand in his. Suddenly, he sat up in the bed as if the cocked spring of a mousetrap had been triggered. Perspiration was pouring out of his pores and covering his whole body like the morning dew that covers God's green earth. His eyes were wide open, and he could feel the adrenaline pumping through his veins telling his brain to signal his reflexes to fight or run.

Looking around the small dimly lit room for some invisible intruder, he began to slow his breathing. As he slowly recognized his own bedroom, he realized that once again he had been transported to another place in time that he wished he could put to rest. Just then he felt his face and arms and the welts that were always with him. With great sadness, he realized that as long as he had these scars, he would always remember. And even if he were able to somehow forget, he knew that the eyes of others who looked upon him would always be like mirrors that never lie.

As the perspiration still poured out of his pores like blood from an open wound and into his eyes, he felt the burning sensation blurring his vision. As he wiped his eyes with the coverings of his bed, he noticed through the thin veil of needlework draping the windows that the storm was raging outside. The snow falling heavily looked like confetti cascading down on a hero's welcome home parade. Reaching for the lamp beside his bed, he felt the chain as it hung from the lamp. Pulling the chain, a click brought forth the light. He threw back the covers and swung his feet around until they lightly touched the cold, hard, wooden floor. Briskly rubbing his hands and arms for warmth, he searched for a pair of lamb's wool slippers and a flannel house robe. After tying his robe, he moved into the den to check the wood-burning stove. He had brought in plenty of wood the day before, so he opened the stove's front hatch and stoked the few remaining coals with about four pieces of wood.

Taking advantage of the time, he sat back in his worn-out chair and took his Bible from its resting place. He really loved this old Bible. It had been a gift to him on that special day—a day that always brought a smile to his face and a sense of failure in his being. Opening the frail cover to the inside page, he read the words that represented the hopes and prayers of so many for his life.

Dear Caleb,

Please accept this Bible as a gift from all those who are praying for you. We know God is with you and that He has great plans for your life. There will be good times, sad times, and some hard times as you endeavor upon the path that God has for your life. Always remember that God is in control, and He is on His throne. May He truly bless you as you follow Him in missi . . .

Suddenly, he felt her presence in the room, and closing the Bible quickly, he turned to see Joy standing in the doorway.

"How long have you been up?" They both questioned each other in chorus.

Both became silent for a moment as if testing the other to see who would answer first. "I thought I heard noises, so I came in here as you were putting wood in the stove," Joy said.

Being a private person, he knew she would have also seen him reading the salutation in his Bible, and this made him give an answer to which no question had been asked. "Sometimes, I like to read before I start my day," Caleb said.

"Nothing wrong with that. What are you reading?" Joy asked.

"Just a letter from some old friends," he answered as he put his Bible away. He did not want to give her any more ammunition to use against him the next time she became anxious.

"Looks like a Bible to me," she replied loftily.

"And what if it is?" was his response with a hint of annoyance in his voice.

"Surely you don't believe all that stuff about God's love and forgiveness, do you?" Silence filled the den as he looked, not at her, but through her. He thought to himself, "Now that is definitely the question of all questions, isn't it?" He had asked himself that very question so many times that he had lost count. Did he still believe God loved him? That God died for him? That God was real or that He was in control? That God still had a purpose for his life? Then he heard the words come out of his mouth, "I don't know."

There was a long pause that begged for further information. "There was a time I did believe it all, but it is not as easy as it used to be. I guess I still read it to remind myself of better times. Old habits, even good ones, are hard to break."

At that very moment, Joy knew this man, Caleb, would never harm her. Suddenly, she was not afraid to be in this stranger's house—maybe because he was not such a stranger after all.

She could sense in his voice as well as in his look of solemn regret, that he had been hurt inside as well as outside. She wondered if this was the time to ask the one question that had plagued her mind since she first saw him. What happened to him that gave him those deep scars? She could no longer stop herself from looking, staring, and wondering about them. But her journalistic instincts warned her that it was not yet time to even approach that bridge, much less walk on it.

Just then Joy heard the howling wind. It was like a solo in a foreboding requiem mass. The early morning light had begun to paint the edges of the earth as it moved up into the sky. Joy, having wrapped herself in a soft blanket, sat down on the sofa and gently pulled her legs up into the warming protection of the blanket.

As if her knowing did not matter anymore, he pulled out his Bible once again, opening it to the letter. He read the bottom of the page where a verse had been written:

And we know that in all things God works for the good of those who love him, who have been called according to his purpose.
—Romans 8:28

CHAPTER SEVEN
Thankful?

When evening arrived, the strength of the storm was still surging. Caleb busied himself all day trying to keep the wood-burning stove hot enough to combat the cold air that whipped in through the cabin walls.

When the wind became stronger, Joy could hear the whistling that was produced by the wind as it forced itself through the tiny cracks of the walls. It was as if it wanted to be inside too and out of the cold. The chinking between the logs of the cabin had become brittle with age, and some had not been able to withstand the force of the wind from the outside. Joy had only been isolated from civilization for a little more than a day, but already she was worrying about whether cabin fever was beginning to claim her mind. She could not believe the turn of events that had placed her here. She had not bothered to listen to any weather reports when driving from the airport. How could a few miles of elevation and twenty-four hours produce such a change in climate? It was evident that she knew nothing of mountain culture, and this made her begin to second-guess herself. "I should have just taken the freeway," she told herself. "I would be in Asheville by now with my crew." Then she began to realize what she was missing, "Oh, my crew! What about the story?" She couldn't tell which one she was more concerned about. All she knew at this point was that she was at the mercy of this storm, her circumstances, her inability to contact the outside world, and this stranger named Caleb.

One night and almost a whole day had passed. Suddenly, she began to attach a name to him. His name was Caleb, Caleb Nobah. She just could not believe that anyone could ever call him Scarback to his face, but she could see how he had gotten the name. Joy so wanted to know his story about the scars, and then she noticed that they were not as noticeable as before—at least not the ones on his face. However, she still wanted to know what had caused the scars. Joy felt she not only needed to know but also longed to know. Since she could not get to her real story, she was determined to get his story. Nevertheless, she understood that would not happen now.

As she listened to the radio in the den while Caleb was in the kitchen preparing a meal for the evening, she stayed on the sofa elevating her ankle to avoid any unnecessary movement. She knew that when the storm lifted, she would have to go and find help if Caleb would not help her. She also knew that if she was going to get out of these woods with all this snow, she would have to use her injured ankle to walk her way out to the main road to find help. Yet, this did not occupy her mind too much now, for she sensed his gentle and caring spirit. Yes, his spirit. Although it was not what she had expected when she first gasped at the sight of his back and face, deep in her being she sensed that he would help her when the time came.

Just then the announcer on the radio said, "The storm is beginning to move eastward with only scattered flurries dissipating by morning."

"Sounds like good news," she heard Caleb announce from the stove, as he clanged pots and spoons together while stirring the meat that he was cooking for dinner.

Joy began to wonder how much longer it would take for the snow and ice to melt enough to allow travel. Again, her thoughts turned to her crew and the story that she still could not wait to get to the bottom of. She reasoned that they must be worried about her. She also had heard earlier on the radio that Asheville was hit even harder. She hoped that they had been able to find a nice, cozy hotel room. She also hoped that they had been able to follow up on some of the leads by phone or with some of the other guests at the hotel. She played out in her mind what they might be thinking. Joy imagined that they probably thought that she too had found a safe hotel room to hold up in.

Then she asked out loud, "But surely, if that were true, they would be curious as to why they had not received a call from me yet. They must be worried about me, and they have good reason to be."

Caleb, hearing her from the den, assured her, "Everything will be fine soon. We will be able to help you get back to your crew and get to your story. Then under his breath, he mumbled, "Then I can get back to my own life and back to my old routine." Though secretly, he had begun to warm to her and her presence.

"Dinner is served," she heard him announce as the sound of his heavy winter boots cracked the old wooden floor slats while making his way to the den. "I hope you like Italian," Caleb said with a half-smile on his face.

She caught herself noticing his face again—not for the scars as before, but his smile was becoming more obvious. She made a mental note of how inviting it was.

She had begun to lose track for a moment, becoming lost in her thoughts. Then she heard Caleb say, "It's an old family recipe passed down from my grandmother."

Joy shook her head and suddenly was brought back to the present conversation. She said, "Oh, your grandmother?" Seeing a way to find out some answers about Caleb and what happened to him, Joy pressed on, "What was she like?"

Caleb just looked at her as if he really did not believe that she was interested in hearing about his past and that he did not want to get into that at this moment. He handed her a plate of spaghetti and waited for her to take hold of the plate, not saying a word in response to her question.

After another moment of awkward silence, Joy decided to change the subject, "Smells good, thank you." She took the plate and placed it on her lap and began eating. Then she noticed him closing his eyes and bowing his head after he sat down in his chair. With his hands folded together and his food placed on the TV tray before him, he was quiet for just a moment or two, and then he opened his eyes, picked up his knife and fork, and began eating.

"Do you do that often?" she asked.

"What, pray?" he answered her question with another question.

"Well, yeah," she shot back at him as if to say, "Duh!"

Caleb responded matter-of-factly, "Yes, I believe we should be thankful for what we receive."

She began to jump for joy inside because she felt this was a first-class springboard to finding out some things about Caleb. The reporter within her began to salivate at the thought of the hunt for the story once again. She took a deep breath and assertively asked, "But what if what we have received is not so good?"

A pause interrupted the air of civility as he peered at Joy with a puzzling focus. He was waiting for further information as to just what she meant by that comment. "I am sorry that I don't have anything to your liking for dinner this evening," he finally said.

Then Joy exchanged a look of questioning with him, and she apologetically held out her hands and said with embarrassment in her tone, "No, no. The spaghetti is very good. Dinner is not what I am talking about."

"Oh, okay," he sheepishly remarked as he resumed his former posture and expressions.

"No, what I meant was, you said we should be thankful for what we receive, and I was just asking if that includes the bad things that happen to us too?" Joy went on to explain. "I mean, take me for example. Here I am on my way to Asheville hoping to crack open the story that just might prove once and for all my abilities as a journalist. And just because I decide to take the scenic route, I end up wrecking my car, spending the night in a ditch, hurting my ankle, walking two miles in excruciating pain, and now being snowed in with…"

He interrupted her soliloquy, "Yes, go on."

She shamefacedly continued by saying, "Well, you know, a stranger." Joy secretly thought to herself how even the meaning of that word was beginning to seem like it did not suit the way she had begun to see Caleb. He was quickly becoming familiar to her somehow even though she really knew nothing about him to speak of. She knew that he prayed and that his grandmother gave him a recipe for spaghetti, and that was about it.

"To answer your question, yes, I do. I do believe that even the bad can be good," he said rather firmly. "I believe that God can bring good out of the bad situations if He wants to," he continued.

"God," Joy teasingly exclaimed. "You talk as if you know Him. I mean prayer is one thing, but to speak of God as if you have figured Him out . . . isn't that just a little presumptuous?"

Caleb quickly remarked, "I never said I had Him figured out. I just said that I believe He can do good when no good can be seen in us or the circumstances that either come to us or that we bring on ourselves."

Joy paused for a while wondering if she should just go for the one question that had been begging to be answered from the very moment, she noticed his scars. She found herself studying the disfigurement of the skin on his face and again thinking that if he could see the good in whatever happened to him, she wanted to know what it could be. Still, she determined that she needed to wait. She had not yet been impressed that the time was right. She would just let the conversation proceed, and who knows, maybe he would just offer up the answers she sought.

Continuing to eat, "Um, um, this is good," said Joy, as she tried to break the awkwardness of the moment. Not sure of how to continue with the conversation, seeing that they definitely did not agree, Joy decided to tread more lightly and less forcefully, "So . . . what do you think about God and how he is running things down here? I mean, you would admit that there is an awful lot of pain in this world, wouldn't you? How can you understand that God loves us all as they say and yet allows so much pain in this world?"

He hesitated for a moment as if collecting his rebuttal, but it was more than that. Yes, he had even rolled that question over in his own mind more than once or twice too. He wasn't sure of the answer any more than the next person, but he finally spoke up. "I think God has shown the world His love, but He will not hinder man's freedom to choose. We can choose to let Him enter our lives or not." Then Caleb posed a curious question back to Joy, "Who do you mean when you say 'they'?"

"What?" Joy asked with an obvious tone of surprise and puzzlement in her voice. Caleb, sensing he had caught her off guard with this simple question, explained, "You know, you asked before, 'How can God love us all like 'they' say?'"

"Oh yeah, I mean, you know— the church, Christians, His people," Joy said.

"Everyone who says they are on God's team may not necessarily be totally correct in that assumption." Caleb went on to further defend his case. "We must be people of faith, even when we can't understand what God is doing." He almost caught himself reaching up to touch the wounds on his face when he heard the words come out of his mouth, but he did not want to give his inner struggles away that easily. Stopping his hand and gaining his composure, he told Joy, with great humility in his voice, "Yes, Joy, somehow I still do believe." It had been so long since he had been close enough to anyone for them to even ask him about what he believed that he wasn't sure sometimes. Now hearing the words that came out of his own mouth, somehow made him stronger.

"So, you would say God has a plan for our lives, huh?" Joy stated and then waited for an answer.

"Yes, I guess I do," replied Caleb.

"What about forgiveness?" Joy asked. "Do you believe God can forgive any sin?" Joy waited with bated breath to see what he would say to that question.

Caleb continued to lay it all out for Joy so that she might understand, "That is the very reason why Christ came into the world. The Bible says He came so that you and I may believe in God and know that He does forgive us of our sins if we take Him into our lives."

"Any sin?" she quickly replied. "I mean what about adultery, murder, or even abortion?" Joy trusted that she was not revealing too much of herself and began to wonder who was leading the conversation.

"The question you are really asking is whether there is any sin greater than the sacrifice of Christ's life on the cross. And to that question, I have to respond with a no. If I understand the Bible correctly, the only sin that God cannot forgive is the sin that is not confessed. Do you really want to know or are you just trying to make conversation?" he respectfully solicited.

"I am not really sure," Joy said, surprised at her honesty at this point.

Caleb was unsure whether to continue for fear that the message would be mocked by Joy, but he decided to press on by saying, "The Bible teaches that God is a Holy God. He cannot allow sin in His presence. But God also loves His creation, which has sinned and rebelled against Him. To remedy this dilemma, God determined to send Christ as a perfect sacrifice to cleanse all who would repent and turn from the wrongs that they have done against Him. To take Christ as our Savior brings fallen man back into a right relationship with God as it was at the beginning of creation."

Joy had heard all this before and was not sure if she needed to tell him all she had heard growing up or just continue to play the devil's advocate for a while. She thought that maybe Caleb was getting too close to her secrets, and she really wanted to know his inner confidences. Sensing her need to pivot, she decided that for now, she would change the subject and get back to her original quest to learn what had happened to him. She continued by asking, "So, how long have you been living up here in this cabin?"

Discerning her obvious reservations about what he had just told her, Caleb wiped his mouth with his napkin, placed his fork down, and said that he had better get the kitchen cleaned up. He took her finished plate, gathered his dinnerware, and went into the kitchen to begin KP duty.

Joy was left with her own thoughts. She did not want to make Caleb upset with her. He obviously had endured something very painful in his life, and yet, she couldn't identify with his seamless assurance about the things he said he believed.

The storm outside was beginning to move on as the night came in. The room had somehow become warmer than before, and she once again drifted into thoughts of being able to leave soon. She could hear the relaxing sounds of water running in the kitchen as Caleb began washing the remnants left after a good meal.

Joy's thoughts began to gravitate back to Caleb; she reflected on how kind he had been to her. What would make someone do all this for a stranger, especially a stranger who had not been very grateful or even respectful? Joy pondered how he knew more about her than she had been able to learn about him. That did not seem to matter though.

A few minutes later, Caleb came back into the den and went over to the wood-burning stove, opened the front hatch, and placed a few more logs in for the night. Standing up, he turned around and said, "Well, I am going to turn in for the night. Remember that if you need extra blankets, they are in the old chest in the hall. And if you want something else to eat, help yourself to the fridge. Good night, Joy." He left the den and headed off to his room.

Joy lay on the couch as the silence of the cabin engulfed her, thinking over the conversation that had been exchanged at dinner. Caleb had retired to his room about an hour ago, and she began to feel her eyes getting heavy. As she got up to go to her room, she noticed that the coffee table in front of her was an old army footlocker. She thought how strange it was that she had not already noticed it sitting there. Usually, she took stock of everything—it was just in her curious nature to do so. Sitting back down on the sofa, she also noticed it had no lock on it. And on each end, there were latches of some kind, brass in appearance with elongated fasteners that would allow her to access its contents by simply flipping the bottom half up to release its tight hold.

Joy sat there wondering if she would find some of her answers inside. She sat motionless as if staring into the face of a wild animal. She was a very private person herself and would be extremely perturbed if anyone invaded her privacy the way she was thinking about invading Caleb's. Almost as if some other forces were controlling her hand, she reached out her left hand and placed the brass fitting under one finger. Joy pulled up the lid to the trunk slowly and gently. The squeaking sound of aged-old fittings was like the echo of an alarm that had just been tripped. Then the latch gave way to a relaxed position. Now putting out her right hand, she completed the access by flipping up the right latch in the same fashion as the left. Nervously looking over her shoulder for just a moment to ensure she was still alone; she quietly began to remove the objects that were resting on the top of her chest. There was one picture, two large coffee-table books, and a mold of a cabin by a stream. Gingerly prying the lid up, she looked inside at the observable contents. Her eyes opened wide with anticipation as if a treasure had been discovered. At first glance, she noticed a few old books. After picking them up and reading the titles, she realized they were study aids of some kind. Their titles were all related to theology: *The Principles of Expository Preaching*, *The Power of Effective Preaching*, and *The Work of the Pastor is Never Done*. As she brushed some of the dust off, she noticed that near the bottom of the locker was something that looked like the corner of a picture frame sticking out from under some other books. Removing all the books that were on top of the frame, she placed them on the sofa beside her to inspect her bounty. Finally, she removed the last book. She picked up the frame and saw what seemed to be some type of achievement certificate. She held the frame in both hands and then ran her hand across the glass plate to clean off the dust to see the contents, which read:

> "Let it be known that on this day, May the first of 1994, Caleb Nobah Sims has been ordained into the preaching ministry of the gospel of our Lord Jesus Christ."

At first, it did not register to Joy what she was reading. Then, as if a light had switched on, she understood what it was. With great amazement and a sudden knowledge of the irony of this situation, she exclaimed almost loud enough to awaken Caleb, "He's a preacher?" She then caught herself and turned around once again to make sure she had not been spotted. "A preacher! Of all the people that I could be stranded with, I end up with a preacher. Oh, this is rich, God. You must really have a sick sense of humor if you were in control of this whole setup. Well, since the joke is on me, I might as well keep looking for what other kind of cruel joke you have set up for me. At least now I know some answers. But to tell you the truth, I would rather that I did not know this one."

Looking further in the footlocker, she noticed some photos, one of which featured a group of people surrounding a man. Joy decided that this must have been a picture of Caleb and his wife inside a church building. The man was receiving a frame of some kind. Then she put the pieces together that this was Caleb on the day he received his ordination.

Then she asked herself, "He is married? He was married?" This was all too much too soon, and she began to feel the pangs of guilt ring up in her being—the kind that comes when one has been caught doing something that goes against one's own conscience. No one had caught her, yet the guilt had arrived.

Too curious to let go, she looked once more into the box of treasure and found a cassette tape. There was writing on one side that had a label attached to it, and there was a date: October 3, 1994. A title was inscribed on the label as well: "The Fundamentals of the Faith." She thought that this must be a tape of a recorded sermon. She secretly hoped that it was a tape of one of his sermons. Joy had to know what was on the tape, but there was no way she could hear it now. She deposited the tape in her front shirt pocket and decided that she would listen to it later when she was alone. She began to carefully replace the items in the locker, trying very hard to put them in the same order that she had found them. Closing the lid and ever so smoothly securing the latches, she placed all the items back on top of the trunk as they were before she disturbed them from their resting place. As she surveyed the placement of the items, she thought with conviction that no one would ever be the wiser. She anticipated the time, maybe even tomorrow, when she could listen to the tape.

Pushing down the guilt was not as hard as she had thought it would be. After all, she reasoned that she had to be excellent at being sneaky as it was an important skill set for a good reporter. With one more glance around to make sure she had not been spied on, she gathered herself, and with blankets in tow, she limped off toward her bedroom for the night.

As she got ready for bed, she slipped the tape in between the mattress and box springs and turned in for a much-needed rest. Suddenly, the story she was researching in Asheville began to pale in anticipation of what she could find out about Caleb, the preacher. Laying back on the pillow, she started to conjecture all sorts of reasons and possibilities that would have caused him to end up here alone in this cabin. Maybe it was a sex scandal, or maybe he had been caught stealing. Endless thoughts raced through her mind as she slowly fell asleep. Her mind wandered back to a time of pain once again. Only this time it was the events that followed her abortion.

Her father had been gone for two weeks on a business trip. He came home late one evening two days before he was scheduled to arrive back home. Joy was in bed, but hearing his voice downstairs, she got up to greet him when suddenly she heard loud voices exchanging harsh words. She stopped at the top of the stairs and sat down. She could hear her father charging her mother with accusations of insobriety.

"You need help, Lois," he shouted in a harsh and firm tone. "You can't hide all your problems in a bottle."

"Maybe I would not drink so much if you were home more," Joy's mother countered.

"What am I supposed to do, just quit work?" her father demanded. "You better look around, Lois—this house, the cars, the clothes, and the country club. All this costs money, and I must work a lot to give you this stuff," he said defensively.

"Maybe you'd be happier if you didn't even come home," Joy heard her mother say.

Then all she could hear from downstairs were muffled voices as the fight gained in intensity and became more confrontational face-to-face.

Then Joy heard glass shattering as her mother threw the wine bottle and drinking glasses against the hearth of the fireplace. Her mother ran into the hall foyer just beneath the stairs. Looking up, she saw Joy sitting at the top of the stairs with tears streaming down her face. In an attempt to excuse what she knew Joy had just witnessed, her mother said, "It's okay, dear. Just go back to bed; Daddy's home early."

Joy's father came into view. As he looked up at her, he forced a smile on his face. He also tried to console Joy by saying, "It's okay, honey. Daddy's home; just go back to bed, and we will explain in the morning."

Her mother, reached the top of the stairs, took Joy by the hand and pulled her up with a hug. "Come, dear, let me help you get back into bed. You know the doctor told you that you need to make sure you get your rest. Daddy and I are just having a little disagreement, and it will all be better in the morning."

Joy awakened with a burst of fright. She had been dreaming of the night her mother and father decided to separate. Now grown and on her own, the memory of the lies they told her that night filled her with an unforgivable resentment toward her father. Joy recalled that when she went downstairs for breakfast the next morning, her mother was the only one there. She was cooking breakfast, but there were only two plates on the table. Her mother turned around from the stove and just stared at Joy for a while—the kind of quiet glare that always comes before bad news.

"Joy, honey, we are going to be fine," she heard her mother say in a broken voice, trembling with the need to find the right words.

"Where is Daddy?" Joy asked. "Is he still in bed?"

Her mother came closer to try to soften the blow that she knew she had to deliver to her daughter.

Joy instinctively backed away with a firm chin as if to say, "Go ahead and hit me with it." This had been her way of bracing herself to handle bad news.

Joy's mother stood still and said with tears streaming down her cheeks, "He's gone. He has left us, Honey."

"No, you're lying," Joy shouted. "He would not leave us. We are his family. I did what he wanted and killed my baby. How could he leave me now!" She stood frozen; then her tears turned into wrenching sobs of pain that felt like the agony of losing an only son in war.

Then Joy ran outside to see if her dad's car was gone. The garage was empty on his side. Frantically, she ran back inside and went upstairs to her father and mother's room. She looked in the closets and the drawers for signs of his existence. All gone. All gone. All gone. "He *is* gone," she thought to herself as she fell to the floor, legs crossed in a sitting position as her head sank into the palms of her hands. She cried out, "Why? Why would he do this to me?"

Her mother entered the room. She approached with arms outstretched to hold her daughter, hoping to shield her from the pain of betrayal. Joy remembered that morning as if it were today. She had replayed it all over and over in her mind a thousand times. "How could he do this to us?" was always the question she needed to have answered. Later, they learned that her father had been seeing another woman for six months before he left.

"Hypocrite!" Joy said to herself as she sat up in the bed with her arms bent behind her for support. She was sweating profusely as the adrenaline coursed through her body. The dream always produced in her the drive to make him pay for the pain he had inflicted on her and her mother. Somehow getting back at the church and some of its leaders freed her for a time from the memories that haunted her. It was as if she were able to tangibly give some of the grief that her father had given her back to him. Then slowly her thoughts returned to the story in Asheville.

Remembering the tape and where she hid it, she turned over on her stomach and ran her fingers between the ridges of the mattress and box springs. She was feeling for the thin plastic casing of the cassette that had become one more reason for her obsession. It was still there just where she had placed it, and soon, very soon, she would find out about this so-called preacher man named Caleb Nobah. Yes, she would find out, and the thought of this gave her the strength to make it just a little bit longer in this wilderness cabin with a stranger.

She thought about how Caleb said that God works out all things for our good, and maybe, just maybe, this story might be the one that really lets everyone know who's the best at getting the story. She hoped that maybe God was on her side for a change, and although the wreck and the journey to the cabin had been hard, this could work out for her good. Joy became giddy with excitement. She could not wait to see the look on the faces of her crew members when she brought them this beauty of a story.

CHAPTER EIGHT
Hope

"We need some help over here. This little girl is very upset, and she wants some company," Shelly announced to Lucy, Jay, and Ken.

They all looked at each other and shrugged as Jay said, "Well, if we can't do what we want to do, then we need to do something."

They all agreed and went over to meet Shelly and the little girl. She was about eight and had flowing blonde hair with highlights that shimmered like that of a fairy princess. She was crying and asking where her mother was.

Ken, the kind-hearted teddy bear of the group, was quickly drawn to the side of the little girl. He gently told her, as he brushed back her hair from her forehead, "It's all right. We will wait with you until your mother comes to find you. I am sure she is very close and will be here soon."

The child looked up at Ken and said, as if she could read his mind, "You say that, but you really do not believe it. You are missing someone you care about too, aren't you?"

Ken was taken aback at the insight of this little child and could hardly believe his ears. Still, he felt that he needed to respond to her question. He could also sense that she was very smart. "Why yes, as a matter of fact, we are missing our friend too. She is a reporter, and she has been lost for a couple of days. How long has it been since you saw your mommy?"

The little girl replied, "She didn't mean to lose me. It wasn't her fault, but it has been a very long time now. She needs to know that I am all right."

Jay said to her, "Don't you mean that it just feels like a very long time since you have seen your mom?"

"No, I mean what I said. It has been a very long time," the little girl replied with a straight face. Then she went on to say, "But she will find me. My father is working it all out right now."

Lucy then tried to make sense of what the little girl was saying to them by asking, "Do you know where your father is? Can we take you to him?"

"Yes, I know where my father is, but no, you cannot take me to him. You would have to know him to take me to him, and none of you know him yet. But you will," the little girl replied.

The three of them were totally blown away by the words of this child, but they quickly chalked it up to shock or fear and that she really did not know what she was saying. So collectively and without consorting with one another, they all decided to just take everything she said with a grain of salt and try to make her as comfortable as possible.

Lucy decided that she would interview the little girl to try to lighten the mood. She told the child that she was really a reporter, and she wanted her to tell her story and that maybe they could print it in the paper. The child responded happily to this idea and thought it would be fun, so she agreed.

Lucy, with a brush in her hand, pretended to do an interview with the little girl. She began her questioning with, "We are here at the Soul Harvest Soup Kitchen waiting out the storm of the century, and we have with us here a small child." Putting the pretend mic up to the child's mouth, she inquired, "And what is your name little girl?"

Shyly moving to the makeshift mic, the little girl said, "My name is Hope."

Lucy replied, "Well, Hope, it is a pleasure to make your acquaintance. That is a very pretty name. What is your favorite color?"

"Pink, like the color of a newborn baby," she replied to the question.

"Pink like a newborn baby? How is it that you know so much about the color of newborn babies, little Miss Hope?" Lucy asked in a joking way.

Hope quickly responded with, "Because, where my father is lots of newborn babies come to see him every moment of every day. He loves babies and children. He gives them each a name that means something special to him."

Lucy questioned further, "Is your daddy a baby doctor?"

Hope said, "I guess you could say that, but he is great at a lot of other things too. Like he is a good artist and a good singer as well as a great inventor. Basically, he is good at everything he does. He is undeniably the best at everything he does."

Ken took the microphone to continue the interview and said, "Sounds like you really love your father. I wish I had a little girl who loved me as much as you love your dad."

Hope looked at Ken as though she were looking through him and said, "You will later. But your first baby will have to go and live with my father. He will take good care of her until you get there."

Ken was in utter shock at her words. Even though he did not understand fully, he wanted to. So, he asked, "Hope, where is 'there,' so I can come and get my little girl when it is time for her to come home."

Hope responded by saying, "Home is there, but you will not be able to get her until you find where my daddy lives."

By this time, they were all scratching their heads and had no idea what this little girl named Hope was talking about. They wondered if she had been brainwashed or if she was sick. They honestly did not know, but they were intrigued by her and had promised her that they would stay with her while she was waiting for her mother and father to find her. They all just hoped that the little girl would be able to snap out of whatever dream world she seemed to be so deeply lost in.

Lucy asked Hope if she was hungry. Hope told her, "No," but she would like for one of them to read to her.

Lucy said, "Sure, I will read to you, Honey, but the only book I see here is a Bible. I am not sure about everything that is in here. I am in a kind of Buddhist slash Stargazer religion. This Bible might mess up my Karma or something, you know?"

Hope said to Lucy, "I have never understood why so many people will worship the stars and ordinary people rather than worship the One who created people and the stars themselves. Besides, my dad says that if Karma were real, we would all come back as something lower than we were before because no matter how hard we try to do something right, we always mess it up."

Lucy looked at Hope with her eyes opened wide in amazement and curiosity as she nodded and said sarcastically, "I can hardly wait to meet your papa. I bet he must be some character."

Hope said in response, "Oh, you will meet him soon enough, but you might not know who he is when you meet him. He will be a stranger to you."

Lucy found for the first time in her life that she really had no way of getting her mind around what Hope was saying. In the past, she had always known how to take charge of the conversation and guide it where she wanted it to go. And now Hope was doing the exact same thing. Hope knew how to guide the conversation so that she was in the driver's seat, as it were. "Oh well," said Lucy as if giving up, "the Bible it is. Where would like me to read from?"

Hope helped Lucy find Genesis 37 and said, "I love this story about Joseph. His brothers wanted to kill him, but they sold him as a slave instead. They thought they were doing a bad thing to Joseph, but God meant it for good. God is like that. Even the bad things can be good when we let Him work it all out."

Lucy questioned Hope by asking, "Are you sure you want me to read that story? It sounds like it might be a little scary when it comes to the mean brothers and all."

"Oh, no. I love the story. I think you will love it too. One day very soon, you will not only love the story, but you will know that you have actually experienced the truth of the story for yourself. God really does work out all things for our good," Hope further explained.

Lucy looked at Hope with one eyebrow raised in disbelief at what Hope was telling her. She said as she rolled her eyes, "Okay, if you say so."

She began to read about Joseph, how his brothers did not like him, how they plotted to kill him, and then how they sold Joseph into slavery. The whole time Lucy was reading this, she could not believe that this was a Bible story.

She asked Hope, "Are you sure this is right? I thought that the Bible only talked about love and turning the other cheek and stuff like that. There seem to be a lot of bad people in this story. For example, this part where there was no water is horrible. Then they all sat down to eat a meal like they had done nothing wrong. How in the world can all these things work out to be good? And to just sit and eat a meal after hurting someone like nothing ever happened?"

Hope became quiet for a moment as if she were mulling over her thoughts before voicing them. Then she replied calmly, "Lucy, you act as if you have never done anything like this yourself. Like you are shocked at the lack of response of the older brothers to the cries for help from the younger brother. You even seemed surprised that they ate a meal after they had brought harm to the younger brother. Why is this so surprising to you? Do you not remember that you took your friend out to dinner after you took her to the abortion clinic? You thought it might get her mind off everything."

Lucy was in shock and filled with all sorts of emotions like anger and shame as well as disbelief that this child could have known this. She did not know even how to respond. But she was able to keep her calm demeanor and brush the comment aside. She desperately hoped that Ken and Jay would not ask her to explain.

Hope said, "Keep on reading, Lucy. There is much to hope for in the end."

Jay could see that Lucy was rattled and did not wish to torture her any longer by making her read on. So, he said, "Hey Luus, let me read for a little while, so you just listen. You are probably tired after the day we have had."

Jay continued to read about how Joseph was sold into slavery. He read about Joseph as a respected slave in the house of Potiphar and how Joseph was made overseer of his Egyptian master's house, and how the Lord made him prosper because he was faithful to God. But then Jay got to the section of the story that dealt with Potiphar's wife. He wanted to stop and ask a question as Lucy did, but he remembered that Lucy did not like the answer she got. And Jay also knew that he had once been with a married woman, and he definitely did not want that broadcast by this strange little fortuneteller called Hope. He continued with his reading and acted like nothing was going through his mind.

Hope broke into Jay's reading and announced, "I need to go to the bathroom."

Jay let out a sigh of relief and said, "Okay, Honey. It is over there. We will wait for you here."

Hope got out from under the covers of her cot and headed over to the restroom. As she walked toward the bathroom, they saw an eight-year-old walking, but they had all become amazed and convinced that this is no ordinary eight-year-old.

As soon as she was out of their sight and out of hearing range, Ken said, "Don't ask me to read that thing! She and that Bible have some kind of weird psychic connection going on. And by the way, have you all noticed how much she looks like Joy?"

Jay replied, "Yeah, I thought it was crazy, but she really does remind me of Joy a lot, especially her eyes and her hair. Maybe they are related somehow."

Lucy chimed in now that her shock had worn off, "Oh, it would be so cool to get Joy and this kid together. I have never been able to unlock Joy's deep secrets, but this kid could just blurt them out for everyone to hear."

Just then Ken noticed that Hope was returning. He whispers, "Shhh, here she comes."

Hope came back and cozied back into her cot and said, "Okay, I'm back. Please read some more; my favorite part is coming up."

Jay said, "All right, Sweetheart."

He read Genesis 39:20–21, which says, "Joseph's master took him and put him in prison, the place where the king's prisoners were confined. But while Joseph was there in the prison, the LORD was with him; he showed him kindness and granted him favor in the eyes of the prison warden."

Jay could not stand it, he had to ask a question even if it meant he would not like the answer. He ventured out by asking Hope, "If Joseph was innocent and he had found favor with God, then why was he thrown into prison in the first place? God sounds deranged and cruel to me if He would let all this happen to someone who believed in Him and who had always done what was right."

Hope responded to Jay's question by asking another question: "Jay, which do you believe is crueler? To watch someone, starve to death along with their whole family or to put them in prison where they will be fed? Everything that is seen is not always seen as it really is. For example, God sent His Son Jesus to die on the cross. Man saw His Death as His end, but God knew that it was only His beginning. Things that are seen are not always as they really are. I am tired now; I am going to sleep. Good night. Thank you all for staying with me." Hope turned over and closed her eyes and went peacefully off to sleep.

Ken asked, "How does the story end? Read on."

Lucy and Jay agreed that they wanted to know the ending too, so they moved away a little so they would not disturb Hope, and Jay continued reading. He read about the jail and the promises made to Joseph for freedom and how he could tell the meaning of dreams. Then they read how this gift finally afforded him an audience with the Pharaoh.

Lucy said, "I never knew the Bible had cool stories in it like this one. This is better than trying to find out who shot J. R. on *Dallas*. Instead of Joseph's life being one long Sue Ellen dream, he can interpret dreams. Maybe Hope has this same gift. Wouldn't that be cool? Maybe she can help us find Joy."

Ken added his two cents by saying, "Yeah, we will ask her tomorrow. Maybe she can help us. But go on with the story for now; I can't wait to see what happens."

Jay continued to read, "Now Joseph was the governor of the land, the person who sold grain to all its people. So when Joseph's brothers arrived, they bowed down to him with their faces to the ground" (Genesis 42:6).

Lucy broke in and said, "His brothers are going to get it now! They put him in that pit, and he was sold, and he had to go to jail, and now they are in front of him, and they have the gall to ask him for food? This is gonna be good. Get 'em, boy!"

Jay continued to read as Lucy and Ken hung on his every word. "Although Joseph recognized his brothers, they did not recognize him. Then he remembered his dreams about them and said, 'You are spies! You have come to see where our land is unprotected.' 'No, my lord,' they answered. 'Your servants have come to buy food" (Genesis 42:8–10). Jay continued to read for a long while—finally seeing how Joseph forgave his brothers and how he wept at the sight of his father and his baby brother, Benjamin.

Lucy, Ken, and Jay were all amazed at the ending of the story and how beautiful it was to see such utter forgiveness even when someone else does wrong to you. All three of them just sat in silence for a while after they read the entire story, thinking about how the story spoke to certain parts of their own lives that needed to know true forgiveness.

Then Ken said, "What if we are all here for the same reason, not because something is wrong, but because everything is right or will be made right in the end? Do you think that something like that could be possible?"

Jay said, "I don't know, Buddy, but I do know that we are missing two friends that we care about very deeply, and we do not know how to even begin to help them. Maybe there is a God in heaven working everything out. I really do not know, but I hope we find some answers soon."

Just then, Hope turned over and never even opened her eyes. It was obvious that she was still asleep, but she uttered very softly, "Soon, very soon. Everything is not as it appears to be." Then she continued sleeping without the least hint of any obvious disturbance.

Shelly came up at that moment and tapped Ken on the shoulder from behind. He was startled because he was intensely watching Hope sleep to see if she had any other words that might give them a clue. He turned to look Shelly's way and questioned, "Yes?"

Shelly said, "The police are looking for you. They just found your friend Mat, and he is in bad shape. They need to see you and take you to the hospital to sign some papers so Mat can have emergency surgery."

Ken, Lucy, and Jay all jumped up and prepared to follow Shelly. But Shelly stopped them and said, "They can only take one of you; the other two will have to stay here."

Jay went with Shelly to find the police because he was the only one with all the insurance information that the hospital would need. When he got to the officers, he asked an obvious question, "What happened to him?"

The officer said, "He was with the four preachers, and they said he fell off the side of a cliff. The doctors do not know if he will make it. He has gotten some frostbite. It took us a while to get him out of the ravine. It really is bad up there."

Jay, not knowing who to trust at this point and not knowing whether the police were on the side of the four preachers, kept it to himself that Mat was known for being very comfortable on the high snow-filled mountains. He remembered how Mat had won several awards for his pictures taken from high in the Himalayan mountains and how he had to condition himself very hard in survival training just to be considered for such a project. Jay had once again begun to fear for Joy's life and where she might be and also for what might happen to Mat and the rest of the crew at the hands of these men. He tried to think of his next move.

CHAPTER NINE
Heart Exposed

During the night, the snow stopped falling completely. Still, at times the wind would speed through the trees and their branches, and the air filled with fallen snow as if the heavens themselves were sprinkling the earth with mounds of powdered sugar.

Opening his eyes, Caleb sensed the early morning sunshine as it intensified with brightness reflecting off the snow-covered ground. He was not one for sleeping in, but this morning he wished he could take advantage of the warmth that cocooned his body as he lay in bed under the weight of the homemade quilts. Pushing back the covers, the chill snapped at him like a rubber band that had reached beyond its limits. This reminded him that he needed to stoke the wood stove in the den. Gearing up to go outside to refill the near-empty bin inside with wood, Caleb stopped and put the remaining few logs through the hatch on the stove. He then closed the door, and as the metal hinge rubbed against the metal door, it produced a screeching sound that filled the room. As he headed toward the back door, he recalled the stranger who resided just a few feet away from him. He trusted that a quick note left on the table should subdue any fears that might accompany Joy's awakening to an empty cabin. With gloves in hand, Caleb placed a thick stocking cap on his head and rolled it down over his ears; then he took to the snow-covered winter land outside in search of a tree that could spare a few thick branches for cutting into firewood. As the screen door closed behind him, Joy heard the recoiling spring as it pulled the door closed. It made a strong bumping noise, which was then followed by a few lesser ones.

Joy could hear the crunching of boots outside as Caleb began his journey in the snow. Startled by the hope for adventure, she remembered the tape. Getting out of bed, she quickly reached for her clothes, as the heat had not yet reached her room. Pulling on her socks, she carefully rolled up the sock on her right ankle, realizing that the swelling had gone down some, and it was not as tender as before. She muttered something to herself about it not being broken after all. Then crouching down beside the bed, she slid her hand between the mattress and the box springs searching out the spot where she had placed the tape the night before. Finally, her fingers felt the thin sides of the tape, and she managed to grip it with her index and middle fingers, pulling the tape out from its cave to freedom—freedom to tell Joy what had become more than just a need to know; she had begun to envision some dark mystery that she must unravel. From her bedroom door, she could see a note on the table, so she walked over and picked it up, and read: "The storm has passed. The woodbin is empty. I have gone out to find some branches for cutting. Be back in an hour or two."

"Uh," Joy said to herself, "He's not much for conversation in word or letter." Forgetting the letter, Joy dropped it on the table. With the tape in hand, she reminded herself that she had about an hour—maybe even an hour and a half—that she could count on. Knowing that he had just left a few minutes earlier gave her an advantage that she desperately needed. The clock was already ticking, so now was the best time to listen to the tape. Knowing that her time was short, she began to rummage through the house looking for a cassette player; even a Walkman would serve her purposes. Standing in the center of the cabin, which was in the den area right behind the sofa, she looked around trying to imagine where he might have placed a cassette player. The only indication that he might have one was the tape she held in her hand. So, she deduced that he must have had one at some time. As she turned around pointing toward each room, she tried to sense which direction to go. Then, as if guided by a sixth sense, she went back over toward the bedroom she had been staying in. Remembering that she had seen an old rolltop desk in the corner of the room, she went right to it. Opening the top, she saw small boxes of odds and ends in the small box portals. Pulling and pushing the drawers on each side of the desk, she glimpsed a black wire sticking up in the bottom drawer on the left side. As she pulled the wire out, she could see that it split into two strands that were attached to a set of headphones. Digging a little deeper, she caught sight of an old desk cassette player toward the bottom of the drawer. She reached down and grabbed the player and turned it sideways; she maneuvered it from the drawer. Checking underneath to make sure the batteries were in place, she felt as if she had unearthed a hidden treasure. With the player and the headphones in hand, she moved back into the den and sat down on the sofa as she placed the cassette player on the footlocker in front of her. Snapping the headphones into the side outlet of the player, she popped the cassette loader up with the push of a button and slid the tape into position, pushed down the loader, and pressed the rewind button. As the tape began to recoil, it hissed with speed as Joy felt the rush of anticipation. This could give her insight into Caleb's true identity. She looked out the front window to check for any signs of his early return. Suddenly, she realized the snow had stopped and the sun was almost blinding to her eyes as it reflected off the snow on the ground.

Then it dawned on her that she normally would be chomping at the bit to get out of there. But now that the storm had let up, she somehow felt okay with taking her time if she could get the story that was before her.

"Click." The player sounds told Joy that the tape was ready to be played. After she pushed the Play button, she parked herself back on the sofa, placed the headphones on her head, and waited for the sound to begin.

Then a voice came over the headphones that she recognized immediately. "If you have your Bibles with you this morning, please get them out and turn to the Gospel of John, chapter fourteen, looking at verse six."

Joy looked over toward Caleb's chair, noticed his Bible, stopped the tape, and went over to pick it up. After she returned to the sofa, she started the tape again and opened the Bible to the assigned place, and followed along as he began the sermon.

"In the Gospel of John here, we see where Christ declares Himself to be the only way to have a relationship with God the Father. This is not popular today. Today, many want a religion in which they can pick and choose what they want. They pick a faith as if they were at an all-you-can-eat buffet. They want lots of forgiveness, a lot of love, throw in some compassion but not too much, and a little morality for good measure. But stay away from discipleship, loving your enemies, becoming Christlike, or giving up anything that displeases us. And whatever we do, don't ask us to partake of the dish called 'suffering for the kingdom of God.'"

Joy listened closely to every word, not sure what any of it meant. She had a transfixed look on her face as the tape kept rolling. She tried to understand; she really did because something or someone was tugging at her heart. She was curiously being drawn in like a moth to a flame, but she did not want to get burned. The message she was hearing was not like any sermon she had heard when she used to go to church as a young girl. She never heard a preacher talk about suffering. And what was all the talk about loving your enemies? But what most intrigued her was the part about a kingdom, the Kingdom of God.

The sermon continued with Caleb reading John 10:10: "The thief comes only to steal and kill and destroy; I have come that they may have life and have it to the full." As fast as her fingers could turn the thin pages of the Bible, she found John 10:10. As she continued to listen, she heard Caleb speak about John 14:6, which says: "Jesus answered, 'I am the way and the truth and the life. No one comes to the Father except through me.'"

She could not understand what she was hearing, but somehow, she felt an attraction to and resistance to these words, all at the same time.

"Jesus said if any man would come after Him he must be willing to take up his cross and follow Him daily. Today's church wants to make it easy for anyone to come to God—to come without commitment that is, without allowing Christ to be the Lord of their lives. Christians today want the benefit of the assurance of salvation without the Cross, without repentance, and without working toward being Holy."

Joy's mind began to wonder about these words. What did repentance mean? What was salvation all about, and how did one carry a cross every day? These questions began to plant in her a drive she had never known before. She was more than just curious. She wanted to know what was meant by the words of this man on the tape. Did he still know what was being taught on this tape? Could he tell her what was being said if she asked him? A strange sensation was running through her. She must find out what all of this meant, but how?

"Jesus said that every person will have to give an account to Him on the Day of Judgment. In Philippians, chapter two, the apostle Paul wrote that the day is coming when every knee will bow and every tongue will confess that Jesus Christ is Lord to the glory of God the Father."

Joy was following the sermon along with each new Bible verse Caleb mentioned. She was caught up in the message. She could not explain it, but these words were stirring her heart, her very being—deep down in her soul.

The message continued: "Many now want to try to live the Christian life in their own strength, in their own power. But they are failures because they do not let God take complete control of their life and heart. Jesus said we must be willing to turn from our sin, repent, and be truly sorry for breaking God's Holy commands. He said we must receive Him into our hearts as Lord and as Savior. We must come to God on His terms, not man's terms. There is no other way to have peace with God, with others, or with ourselves. Paul wrote in Romans 10:9 that 'If you declare with your mouth, 'Jesus is Lord,' and believe in your heart that God raised him from the dead, you will be saved."

Joy repeated the words that stood out the most, "Peace with God, peace with others, and peace with oneself." Joy knew that this was what she had wanted for so long. She had given up on ever finding the peace that was being discussed in this sermon. She began to understand some of it. She understood a little about what repentance meant from listening to the words on the tape. But how could one take Christ into their heart?

She still wasn't sure what salvation was or even why she needed it, but she wanted to know. John 6:44 says, "No one can come to me unless the Father who sent me draws them, and I will raise them up at the last day." Joy began to question, "Is this happening to me right now? Is this the Father drawing me in? She knew her life was missing something. She could sense it. She knew that things were not exactly right with her and for that fact, maybe never had been right. She didn't have the power to forgive herself. Then she thought that surely God couldn't ever forgive her for the dreadful sin of killing her own child in an abortion. She reflected on how she had heard a lot of salesmen in her life, and she had learned the hard way that when something sounds too good to be true, it usually is. Still, she wanted to forgive her dad, she wanted to forgive Brad, she wanted to forgive her mother, and most of all she wanted to forgive herself for the part she had played. Maybe it was just too late for her. She listened more as the voice was booming in her ears with an assurance that anyone could come if only, they would come.

"People throughout time have thought that God would not accept them. But we need not listen to the enemy of our souls, the devil, any longer. Jesus said in John 6:37, "All those the Father gives me will come to me, and whoever comes to me I will never drive away." Oh friend, do not delay. If you hear God speaking to your heart today, then come and ask Him for a new life. Ask Him to forgive you of your sin, to cleanse you from all unrighteousness. Ask Him to come into your heart today before it is too late. In 2 Corinthians 6:2, Paul wrote: "In the time of my favor I heard you, and in the day of salvation I helped you. I tell you, now is the time of God's favor, now is the day of salvation."

The tape kept playing as the message came to a climax, asking people to come forward and make a public profession and commit their lives to Christ. When the sermon was over, Joy pressed the Stop button and sat there quietly trying to take in all that she had just heard.

Suddenly, she felt she was the one that was being searched out. She was the one being exposed. Something had touched her inside, and it made her feel once again like she was not in control. She sensed it was time to put everything away for now. It had been over an hour since Caleb left the cabin, and she must put the player and the tape back before he returned. This thought sent a sudden surge of energy through her body. She got up quickly and took the cassette player back to her room and placed it in the bottom drawer just as she had found it. Then moving back into the den, she sat down on the sofa and moved the pictures from atop the footlocker. Popping the latches and opening the top, she moved some books out of the way and placed the tape near the bottom. Just as she was about to put the books back in the trunk, two letters fell out from inside the dust jacket of one of them. Then she heard a noise coming from outside. "Caleb," she thought, "he's back." Now the letters had sparked another note of curiosity. Quickly placing them inside her shirt, she grabbed the remaining books and tossed them in the locker. She closed the lid, snapped the latches down, and placed the pictures back on top.

Then she heard the spring on the back door groaning as it stretched to allow Caleb's entrance into the cabin. As he came through the door, Joy noticed that his stocking cap was snow-covered and his boots were wet from melted ice. He stomped his feet to knock off the snow residue, and with one quick gesture of his hand, he freed his head from the stocking cap.

Seeing her sitting there on the couch, he cheerfully said to her, "Well, good morning. Did you sleep well last night?"

"Okay, I guess," Joy responded.

"How's that ankle today?" he asked.

"Oh, it seems to be doing much better. I can put a little weight on it now," she said.

"That's good, I believe I was able to scrounge up enough wood to last a day or so. Maybe by then, the ice will have given way enough to find more," he told Joy.

"Well, I umm," Joy was hesitant to bring it up, "I was thinking if the weather held out that maybe you could get me down to a phone or something. My crew must be going crazy by now, and they are probably out searching for me."

"Oh yeah, sure," Caleb answered.

Then it hit him. Even though he did not let on to Joy at all, he really had begun to regret the thought of her leaving, and he did not know why. He knew he wasn't falling for her, yet it was nice to have someone else around, even if she were a bit high-minded and tended to believe that she was always right. He told himself again that he wasn't becoming attracted to her, but still, there was something about her. She reminded him of someone. He walked into the kitchen to start preparing their lunch, but he could not stop wondering who she reminded him of. Then it dawned on him as surely as the morning sunshine. It was Joy's spirit, her energy, and her blond hair. Why had he not seen it before? He began to think back to another time.

Caleb had never been one to let anyone in. But this was different. He had met her at college Bible study. He remembered when he first met Sandy. She didn't catch his attention too much at first. Then it was she who kind of singled him out. She just sat there beside the lamp in the corner of the room waiting for the Bible study to begin. The leader of the study announced Caleb to the group and expressed how glad everyone was that he could make it. Caleb had already felt the warmth of acceptance from the group since he knew some of the members from a previous school. Here he was a member of a family of friends; they didn't judge him or his appearance. He found himself sitting on the floor next to where Sandy was seated on a chair. As the study began, Caleb contributed much to the discussion. This was one subject he knew a little bit about. He had always been interested in theology and what it meant to follow God.

Sandy was dressed like a backpacker. He could tell right off that she was down-to-earth, a nature lover. He had a name for people like her, "Granola Heads." He didn't mean anything by the name. It just helped him to categorize people in his mind, so he would know how to talk to them. After that night Sandy began to sit with him at lunchtime, and he felt very comfortable with her. She seemed to be a lot like him. They began to go out as friends, and when they had money, they would often go into town to eat at the local pizza shack. They would spend hours there just talking mostly. She said she wanted to be a missionary. He often wondered what kind of a person would want to do that with their life.

She wasn't like any girl he had ever met. He could talk to her, and she enjoyed listening to him when he talked about God. After they came back from Christmas break during their first year at school, something began to change. She started talking about how much she had missed him over the holidays. Soon they were going out even more and seeing each other as much as they could after class, after lunch, and in the evening. The evening was the time when they would just sit in his car and talk sometimes till one or two o'clock in the morning. And they would even do this on the weeknights. Then one night as they were just sitting in his car, she told him that if he wanted to, he could kiss her. He froze at first, thinking she was joking or playing some kind of pity game on him.

But then she leaned over toward him, and he kissed her. Caleb thought to himself, "Well, there were no flashes of light or fireworks. But something had happened. Could it be that Sandy really was attracted to him? Was it possible she did not notice the scars? Or maybe she had a way to look past them?"

She made him feel like a better person than he had thought of himself previously. After that night they began to see each other even more, but this time it wasn't just as friends.

Months went by and again she was the one who approached the subject one evening. They had gone to a nearby park for a picnic, and afterward, they began to wrestle as lovers do. As he had her pinned down to the ground, she looked up at him with her eyes meeting his and ever so quietly said, "If you were to ask me to marry you, I would say yes."

He just looked at her deep into her eyes, searching out the possibility of a terrible prank being played on him. But what he saw was a smile across her face that told him that somehow, she meant what she said. That made him happy, and he did ask her to marry him. They began to make plans to marry after they graduated in a year. All their friends were happy for them. They seemed strangely the perfect couple for each other. Caleb had not met her parents yet. The subject came up one night that they should go to her home for the weekend, and he would ask for her parent's approval for them to marry. It was also at this time that he began to feel the call of God on his life to go into the ministry.

Sandy had opted for a life with him instead of going to the mission field. He had shared with her one night how he was changing directions and would apply to seminary after graduation. Up until that time he had dreamed of being a psychologist. He always wanted to help people with their problems, and now God had called him to do it for His Kingdom.

It was Spring Break. He and Sandy had decided they would go to her home to finally meet her parents. He borrowed a friend's car to make the trip fearing that his car would not make the journey. The road trip was great fun for them both. As they reached the city that evening, Sandy began to give him directions to her home. As he continued to follow her guidance, he began to see that the houses that he passed were all in a very ritzy neighborhood. He kept quiet, but a sense of feeling out-of-place began to swell up within him.

"There it is on the corner," Sandy said with excitement.

Caleb was very nervous. The house was very big. A large boat was parked in the massive driveway. He knew that Sandy had not told him everything. He stopped the car, put it in park, and shut it off. He got out and opened the back door to get their bags.

As they approached the walkway that led to the front door, Sandy stopped and turned toward him, and said, "Are you ready? Here let me fix that." Sandy ran her fingers through his hair trying to tidy him up a bit. "Tuck your shirt in," she told him instead of asking. She was a little different unexpectedly.

He wanted to just get back into the car and leave. He didn't know this, Sandy. He wished that they could just get in the car and go back. Go back to the way it was just fifteen minutes ago, but it was too late. Sandy opened the front door and ran inside leaving him at the door to manage three bags. Making his way through the entrance, he was carrying their luggage when a tall, slender woman with gray-peppered hair met him in the foyer.

She paused for a moment and caught herself staring at Caleb. He knew that look; he had seen it literally a million times. He saw it every time he met a new person or anyone on the street just passing him by. "No, no, no," were her first words to Caleb. "Don't put those bags down there. Go ahead and take them into your room."

Caleb reached down once more, feeling more like a butler than a guest, and took the bags to the front room, just off the den. He closed the door behind him as he placed the bags on the bed. He sat down on the bed for a moment and asked himself what he was doing there. Caleb had come from a very different family, to say the least. His father had worked in a cotton mill all his life and hated every day of it, taking out his misery on the kids and the bottle. His mother had never finished high school and married just to get away from home. Talk about jumping out of the frying pan into the fire. The only way Caleb had been able to go to college was because he had a grandmother who had always told him that if he could get into college and if he wanted to go, she would pay for it. Well, she did help for the first two years, but then he had to find odd jobs and get student loans to continue his junior year.

"Knock, knock," Sandy said as she opened his bedroom door. "What are you doing in here? Come on out. I want you to meet Daddy."

Caleb followed her into the dining room where her mother had dinner waiting on the table. "You kids come on and sit down before everything gets cold." Sandy's mother summoned.

As everyone sat down, Sandy's father made his grand entrance and found his way to the chair at the head of the table; he began talking to Caleb even before he looked up at him. He then sat down in his chair, still not having looked at Caleb.

"Well, Caleb, how are you treating my little girl?" Sandy's father, Tom, asked as he placed a napkin in his lap.

"Pretty good, I hope, Sir," Caleb answered.

Just then Tom looked up at Caleb for the first time and paused just a moment as a look of confusion went across his face.

"You'll have to do better than pretty good," Tom said as he looked around the table to see if anyone else had caught his subtle joke.

Sitting there for what seemed like hours, the conversation was mainly between Sandy and her parents. They talked about school, classes, grades, and whether Sandy had given up on that silly notion of being a missionary. Toward the end of dinner when everyone had gotten quiet, Sandy motioned with her eyes and with the tilting of her head that now was the time to speak to her father about their plans.

Caleb nodded in agreement but was not sure of any plans right now. Clearing his throat as he put his fork down and placed the napkin beside his plate, Caleb began to speak.

"Um . . . Mr. Dingle," calling Sandy's father by his surname and indicating that the mood was changing to a more serious matter. He nervously continued, "Sandy has given up the notion, silly as you say, about becoming a missionary."

Immediately Tom looked over at Sandy and expressed his pleasure with a big toothy smile.

"Sandy and I have been seeing each other for some time, and we have made some plans that we would like to share with the two of you."

"Oh, and what might these plans consist of?" Tom asked with a flippant tone, the kind of tone an adult uses when explaining adult stuff to children.

"Well . . . we love each other very much, and we believe God has brought us together. We want to get married," Caleb blurted the last part, not quite believing he had said it.

Tom placed his long-neck beer bottle down on the table and just looked at Sandy. Her mother reached over to cup her daughter's hand as it rested on the table. This was Mrs. Dingle's way of trying to keep everyone quiet so that Mr. Dingle could have his say without being interrupted. Sandy had been conditioned since she was a little girl to know what her mother's hand gesture meant.

"Sandy, is this true?" he asked his daughter.

Sandy, feeling the atmosphere turning sour, looked over at Caleb. After a long silence, she said, "Yes, Daddy, it's true."

Tom went into a long story about how he and Mrs. Dingle had gotten married years ago. He told Caleb how difficult it was when they got married, how he was just a private in the army, and how on the day they were married, all they could afford was a bus ride to a hotel for two nights for a honeymoon trip. He lingered on about making "his way" in this world, how his business had failed earlier in life and that today young people don't look down the road at all the obstacles before them.

He turned to Sandy and began to question her about her plans for school.

Caleb tried to interrupt and explain that they are thinking about some of these questions, and they are planning to stay in school and not marry until after next year's graduation.

Then Tom turned to Caleb and asked, "What then?" Looking in Caleb's direction, "What then? I mean what do you plan to do, Caleb?"

Caleb began to feel a defensiveness going through his voice as he tried to answer the question. "I was planning on becoming a psychologist or a counselor to help people, but now I know that God has called me to the ministry. And after graduation, I plan to go to seminary to prepare for that life. I know it will be tough, but with God's help, I know we can make it."

Almost as if the entire scene had been previously choreographed, Tom shouted back at Caleb's defense and said, with a definite tone of judgment, "A minister? You will never make enough money to keep our Sandy in the lifestyle that I have afforded her."

CHAPTER TEN
Jesus Freak

"Ouch!" Caleb said loudly as the crimson liquid streamed down his finger. He had become so engrossed in thought that he had cut his index finger as he sliced a tomato for the salad he was preparing for lunch. At the sink he grabbed a white kitchen towel and ran cool water over the injured finger; he sized up the divide of flesh as his finger kept bleeding. He pressed the towel on the cut and held it there for a moment to stop the bleeding. He looked for a bandage under the sink where an old first aid kit was stashed among the clutter. Having located the kit, he popped the latches and with his unharmed hand, he lifted the top and picked up a small roll of gauze. Holding the towel in place with his thumb, he opened the gauze roll and began to wrap the wound in a circular motion around his finger. He then secured the makeshift bandage with a piece of white tape and discarded the bloody towel in the dry side of the sink. Returning to his lunch preparations, he once again found himself thinking back to that night when he met Sandy's parents. He remembered that it was her father who had left a cut in his pride and his soul that still unnerved him every time he recalled that night.

It was more than just the words her father used that evening that stuck with him. It was what had been clearly implied that still registers a deep emotional wound even to this day. It was communicated that Caleb was not good enough for them—not just for Sandy, but not good enough for any of them. Tom certainly made it clear that his daughter would not be happy being married to a seminary student and certainly not to a minister. It was more than the lack of money that was standing in Caleb and Sandy's way of marriage; it was the clash of values about God and who He should be in one's life as well. Tom felt that God was only good for fire insurance. He believed that a prosperous life on earth was gained only by hard work and luck, not by God and his blessings. It was made obvious to Caleb that Sandy was Tom's daughter first and foremost and that one day he would decide who she would marry and what kind of life she would live. And he was definitely opposed to the thought of her marrying some "Jesus freak."

After that night, he and Sandy were not the same. She didn't say it as much as she showed it. Her father had disapproved of Caleb, and as time went on, she too would find it harder to leave her parents and cleave to Caleb, as it were.

That night was just the beginning; it would be two long days before he and Sandy would leave to go back to school. The strangest day was Sunday morning. The family got up early to get ready for church; on the drive there, Sandy and Caleb sat in the back seat of the family car like two children on a vacation trip. It was as if Tom was oblivious to the Friday evening meal and their conversation; he talked about this new car and how he was looking forward to taking out his new boat for a Sunday afternoon cruise at the nearby lake.

Caleb just sat in the back seat occasionally looking over at Sandy as she and her parents conversed about all the latest town events. Their conversation was mostly gossip—small talk about who had lost their job or who was building what house or even who was involved in an affair. Caleb thought to himself that this was not a very good example of uplifting Christlike conversation. In his mind, it was cruel to tear down the same people that you worship with. He saw the hypocrisy. When they arrived at the church, Tom parked the car, and everyone got out to go inside. Tom spoke to everyone and proudly displayed his ability to hobnob with the fine church folk.

Caleb felt that the service was as cold as an ice rink, and never a word was said during the sermon about Christ and what He had done for humanity on Calvary. After the service, they went to a nice restaurant and ate Sunday dinner together. Again, only small talk was discussed between them. Caleb could only wonder why Sandy had not even once tried to dispel her father's disapproval of their plans. It was as if once her father gave his order, that was it. And so, it was.

When they arrived back at the house, Sandy and Caleb began to pack and prepare for the drive back to school. After all the goodbyes were said and Caleb attempted to give Tom a firm handshake, Caleb got into his borrowed car and waited for Sandy to join him. All the way back, they just looked out at the scenery, because the atmosphere would not allow any questions and certainly not any answers. Caleb could feel that it was over, but he still wanted answers. It wasn't official though until after that semester when Sandy began to mention something about going to another university the following fall. Caleb was supposed to believe that they would still see each other and that she was going because of the challenge she would receive. She also said she had friends there that she wanted to be close to again.

That summer Caleb called Sandy one night from a friend's apartment—the same friend he had borrowed the car from—and told Sandy that he did not want to get married. The feeling was mutual, but still Sandy seemed to struggle with the idea that he was breaking it off with her. It was almost as if she couldn't believe he could let go of her, although she had long since let go of him. Now though, it was official, but Caleb did see Sandy one more time.

Later that fall, Sandy came for a weekend to see some girlfriends in their dorm, and she and Caleb met one evening and even talked about getting back together. But after Sandy went back to her school, Caleb received a letter about two weeks later explaining that she had met someone else. A guy named Norman. Caleb never even wrote back. He tossed the letter in the trash even before he left the post office. He knew it was Sandy's way of saying she had broken up with him. Somehow, he didn't care; he was just relieved that it was over. He chuckled a bit as he left the post office thinking of the name of her new beau: Norman. Sounded almost like "Normal" to him, but he knew any life with her would be anything but normal.

Thinking back on that whole experience, even to this day, it was never Sandy that caused Caleb to feel the pain of that relationship. It did not bother him at all anymore that he didn't marry Sandy. He was glad in fact. Later, he heard that Sandy and "Normal" got married and had seven children.

"Whew," he would always murmur to himself; he knew he made the right decision, or she did. He loved his solitude and quiet time too much to believe he would have been a good father. No, it was not Sandy that still hurt him; it was the words of her father although Caleb never could pinpoint exactly why. The thought of being inferior to Tom was still an open wound even now. Could it be because he felt the rejection of another man who could have represented a father's forgiveness to him? Was it because he felt inside the truth of what those words told him? That he really wasn't good enough for this rich man's daughter? There was a time in Caleb's life when he felt that he knew something the world did not know. Something about being close to God and that having God made one rich. But this one man, Tom, had undercut that childlike belief in Caleb to its very core—not by causing Caleb to lose his faith, but by causing him to lose his self-confidence.

At one time Sandy had made him feel as though the visible scars he carried didn't matter. Even Tom never mentioned his appearance. It was more internal. It was almost as if Tom could sense the kind of family Caleb had come from and that he was being rejected based on whose he was and not just who he was. Two men now had rejected Caleb, his own father, and Sandy's father, Tom. Somehow, he wondered whether there was a connection there that he just could not see.

"What's for lunch?" Joy asked as she made her way to the door opening in the kitchen.

"Oh, just making a salad and heating up some soup," Caleb said.

"What happened to your hand?" Joy said as she noticed the bandage.

"I cut my finger while I was slicing a tomato. I cleaned it up well though. There should be no worries about contamination," Caleb said in a kind of joking way.

"Oh, Caleb, I'm not worried," Joy laughingly said, but at the same time, she wondered where that came from.

Caleb always had a way of defending himself to others as if they were inspecting him. He had a suspicion of others, and this carried over into any relationship he had with anybody. He always felt a need to perform when around others, and this showed up in different ways.

"Well, I am going back into the den. Call me if I can help with anything," Joy remarked.

"You said earlier that you were hoping you could make plans soon to leave, is that right?" Caleb questioned as he moved over to the stove to turn the heat down on the soup.

"Yeah, that's right. My crew has got to be worried, and I've got to call the rental agency about the car. Oh my, I never mentioned it, but right before I ran the car off the road, I could have sworn I saw a little girl who just seemed to appear in the middle of the road. She couldn't have been any older than about seven or eight. She had long blonde hair, and I think she had on some kind of dress. Later when I awoke from passing out, I went back up to the road to find her. There was no evidence of anything to prove that I had even seen her. I was afraid that I had hit her when I swerved and that she needed help too, but nothing. I first thought that maybe an ambulance had picked her up or someone else, but that did not make any sense either. I thought if that had happened, surely, I would have been found too. I left skid marks all over the road where I lost control of the car. Do you know of any little girls that fit that description around here?"

"The only family that has children around here is the Matthews. But they live about four miles up on the road, and the only children they have are three boys: one redhead and two with brown hair." Caleb responded with a quizzical look across his face.

"Um," Joy mused. Then she moved back toward the den while searching her memory to examine whether she had really seen the little girl at all or just imagined her. "Maybe it was just the sun's reflection of some kind," she said aloud to herself as she sat back down on the sofa.

This in itself was not like Joy. She was not the type to ever second-guess herself. Sitting there for a moment or two, she went over the events again in her mind. She went through a step-by-step progression of the time from when she left the ramp until she skidded off the road into the ditch.

Just then she noticed in the corner of her left eye the corners of the white envelopes she had placed hurriedly in her shirt pocket. They were trying to make their escape out from under the jacket she had on over her shirt. She quickly tucked them back down and raised the jacket zipper a few inches to secure the letters before joining Caleb for lunch.

"Lunch is ready! Do you want to eat in here, or do you want me to bring it into the den for you?" Joy heard Caleb say.

"I'll be in there in just a minute," she called back.

Joy raised herself once again from the couch and made a mental note to try to read the letters as soon as possible. She still felt uneasy about her little plot, but the journalist in her would not subside or retreat.

CHAPTER ELEVEN
Mat

"Okay, Buddy, we are here," the officer said. Jay was startled from his daydreaming about what might be around the next corner. He did not know if Mat was alive or even if any of them would live to tell the story of these four men and the events that had surrounded this terrible storm. He had received word that his boss had been unable to locate Joy. The last they knew of her was that she had rented a car and stopped off at a local station shortly after that. Other than that, no one had a clue. And now he feared that the local police were in on a full-blown cover-up for these men and that his entire crew might not be alive tomorrow.

He got out of the car to go with the police even though he really doubted that they were taking him to Mat as they had said. But he knew he had to go with them just the same—he needed answers. He had always been the one who held everyone together and took care of the details, but this was one time that he felt he was really letting his coworkers down. He was afraid to trust anyone. He also remembered the strange little girl named Hope at the shelter—how much she reminded him of Joy.

He followed the officers through the sliding glass doors of the hospital and down a long hall. There were people everywhere who looked as if they were out of energy and out of place. They all seemed to be very tired and in need of some good rest. Then the officers took Jay to a small room at the back of the hall. It looked like a small break room with a table, microwave, and a small fridge. They told him to wait in there and someone would be with him to let him know about his friend. This too was very suspicious to Jay. Why wouldn't they just take him to Mat and let him see Mat with his own eyes? But he was afraid to let on to anyone about his suspicions. Everyone they had interviewed saw these four men as fabulous. They even referred to them as the "Fabulous Four." Jay's mind began to reel at all the possible scenarios that could come out of this journey.

Jay started trying to put some plan into place. He looked around to see if there was a phone in this little room. After finding one, he picked it up to see if it had a dial tone, but it was dead. In frustration, he slammed down the phone and screamed out, "Why am I just waiting in here?"

At that very moment, the two officers entered the door saying, "Whoa, hold on there; we were not gone that long. We had to get approval for you to see him. He is in intensive care, and no one can see him except the staff or his relatives. But since none of his relatives have shown up yet, the staff thinks it would help him to see someone, anyone he knows. But brace yourself. This will not be easy on your eyes. He had an exceedingly bad fall. Are you sure you can handle this?"

"Yes, he is my friend, and he needs me right now. I will put away any fears of shock I might have," Jay says gallantly.

"Okay then, come on." The officer showed Jay to Mat's room.

Jay turned a corner and saw a man in a hospital bed that had both legs in casts and in traction. One arm was also in a cast and in a stirrup to hold it steady. His face was black and blue and swollen almost beyond recognition. He had hundreds of stitches in his chest and some on his neck. His hair was matted and plastered to his head.

A nurse was sitting at the foot of Mat's bed. She motioned Jay to come over and said, "Come on; he needs to hear a familiar voice. It might help him come out of this so he can make it. They say the hearing is the last thing to go; so talk to him, talk to your friend."

Shakily Jay approached the side of Mat's bed, and he could not believe what he was seeing. Mat was almost unrecognizable. But Jay knew that Mat needed to know that he was not alone. Mat needed to hear that Jay was taking care of things, even if Jay felt totally and utterly powerless to do anything of value at this moment.

So, in hopes he could reach Mat, he began to speak to him. "Hey, Buddy. it's me, Jay. I'm here to take care of you and get you back behind the lens of your true love, Cameron. Can you hear me, Mat? Can you speak to me? Everybody is waiting to see you again. The storm is over, and we will be able to go home soon. Mat, if you can hear me, try to move something. Let me know if you are aware that I am here."

Just then, the nurse at the foot of the bed noticed a muscle contraction on her monitor. "Hey, he hears you. Look for a muscle twitch. I see it on the screen."

Jay looked at Mat's free hand and saw that his thumb was twitching. Jay let Mat know that he could see his response. "Hey, Mat. I see your finger moving. Can you control it enough to tap once for yes and twice for no?"

Mat moved his finger one time for yes.

Jay responded quickly with great excitement, "Did you go up the mountain to take pictures of some children?"

Mat moved his finger once for yes.

Jay asked another question, "Have you seen Joy?" Mat's finger moved two times for no.

Jay, realizing that this was a hard strain on Mat, decided to ask just one more question, "Were you with the four preachers on the mountain?"

Mat's finger once again moved one time for yes.

"All right, Buddy, I will take it from here. You just make sure that you get better and come back to us. I do not want you to worry about a thing," Jay said as he tried to console Mat.

The nurse at the foot of Mat's bed grew curious at Jay's last question, so she asked, "Why did you want to know if he was with the four preachers on the mountain?"

Jay, still not knowing who he could trust, replied, "Oh, um, no particular reason, um, that is just what I heard." Lying through his teeth he continued, "I was just wondering if they were hurt too?"

The nurse replied, "No, I do not believe so; they were just in here before you, and they seemed fine. They were the ones that got to him. If it had not been for them, he would still be out there in that terrible cold. And I doubt that anyone could have survived out there, much less your friend with his terrible injuries."

Jay just had to inquire because the question was burning him, "How do you think it is possible for my friend to look like this and the four preachers to be fine and walking around? Didn't they have to go off the same cliff when they went to get Mat? Do you know anything about what happened on that mountain?"

But with hesitation, she responded, "You know, I was thinking the same thing myself. I am new in town, and I do not know a lot of people. I keep my mouth shut, so I can keep my job. But he does look genuinely bad by comparison. The story is that your friend was taking pictures and got too close to the edge and fell off a part of the cliff that was extremely jagged with sharp rocks and branches. The way he looks he must have hit every one of them on the way down. The preachers are saying that they were able to find a safer place to get down the cliff so they could help him. If all that is true, it would explain why your friend looks the way he does, and the preachers are fine. But I would think that at least one of them would have some kind of injury like frostbite or something. I don't know, and I dare not ask. I need this job."

Jay replied with puzzlement, "Well, I don't know what happened, but I will find out. Can I sign a form requesting that no one can see him except me? Not even the preachers!"

"Why yes, but why do you ask such a question?" The nurse appeared confused.

"Do I have to put a reason on the form?" Jay questioned her.

The nurse responded, "Well, no. I was just curious. As I said I am new to town, and I am still learning everyone. All my coworkers love it when these four preachers come to the hospital. They all say that they are a great deal of help when it comes to the children's ward. When those men come in, the children will be good for hours while the preachers read to them and play games. The nurses on that ward say that they use that time to go and catch up on paperwork and things like that. They say that the preachers are a blessing to them during those times."

Jay, not wanting to give away his thoughts, responded shortly, "Just give me a form to sign so that no one can see him but me. I need to go back to the shelter to my other friends, and we need to go and find someone else. Just know that I work for a very powerful paper, and we have our own lawyers. If anyone and I mean anyone, except medical staff is allowed to see him, we will sue this hospital. Is that understood?"

Feeling intimidated the nurse answered and handed him the form to sign, "Yes, Sir— as you wish."

"Thank you, I will be back to see him soon," Jay matter-of-factly told the nurse. He then went to Mat and said, "Buddy, I am going to have to go for now and tie up some loose ends. Then I will come back, and we will see about getting you transferred back home. You hang in there and get well soon. And don't worry, I am taking care of it, all right?"

Jay looked at Mat's finger, and he saw that Mat tapped once for yes.

Although Jay was afraid to leave Mat, he was even more afraid to leave Lucy and Ken at the shelter. So, he took his leave of the room. As he turned the corner of the hall, he had to stop and collect himself for a moment. He knew that he must be wrong, but he was not prepared for all this uncertainty and secrecy. He recapped the situation. There are five people in this crew: one is missing, one is dying in the hospital, and Ken and Lucy are unaccounted for. He feared that even the phones might be bugged, so he was afraid to call his boss and let him in on any of this. He reasoned that if anyone ever found out that they were here to bring down the Fabulous Four, none of them would make it out alive. He pulled himself together once again and went to find the police and let them know that he needed to get back to the shelter.

CHAPTER TWELVE
Protection

"Thanks for the ride, officers," Jay said as he got out in front of the shelter to go and hook back up with Ken and Lucy.

The officer replied, "No problem, glad to help. By the way, the four preachers that we refer to as the Fabulous Four said to tell you that they had a plan to help you meet up with your friend who is lost. I am not sure exactly what they meant, but if those four say they are going to do something, you can bank on it. Nobody better mess with them around this town or there will be you-know-what to pay. Have a nice day now."

Jay's jaw just about dropped off his face; he did not know if the officer realized that he had just threatened Jay and his friends. Jay and his crew thought that the preachers might have kidnapped Joy to keep her quiet. But he could not tell if the officers were just passing on a message or if they were a part of the threat. This whole thing was becoming more than anyone could stand. Since the storm had let up, Jay thought it might be best for the three left standing to try to make it back down the mountain. Maybe once they got back to the office, they could get some outside help. He hated to leave Joy and Mat behind, but he feared that none of them would make it if they did not at least try to get out.

"Jay," Lucy ran to greet him, "How is Mat?"

"He is not good, not good at all. He can only move his thumb to answer a simple yes or no. It really looks like we are in great danger too. The policemen that dropped me off gave me a threatening message from the Fabulous Four. They said that they were working on a plan to make sure that we would be able to soon meet up with our missing friend."

Ken jumped in, "What in the world do you think that means?"

"I do not know," Jay answered, "And I do not want to stay here and wait to find out. I think we need to put the chains on the tires and try to make it back down the mountain. At least when we get back to home base, we can get some help from the outside. Everyone here is crazy about these men. When I went to the hospital, the nurse told me that these men are even left alone in the children's ward for hours at a time, unsupervised."

Lucy remarked, "You have got to be kidding me! Are these parents crazy? Is there anyone who questions the motives of these men? What in the world have we found up here, and how long has it been going on unchecked?"

Jay said, "I do not know, Luus, but I do know that we are not safe and that we had better get our heads together and come up with a plan."

Ken announced, "Well, it is too late to leave tonight. The temperature has dropped again, and the roads are not safe at all. At least if we stay together and stay in this crowd, then we might have a better chance of being safe. We can go ahead and put the chains on the tires tonight, and then we can leave in the morning after the sun has had a little time to melt some of the ice on the roads. I will see if Shelly will let us have some blankets, food, and water just in case we get stuck. I think we can trust her. She seems to have taken a liking to Mat. She told me that he was helpful when he was here. She has been asking if he is all right."

Jay replied, "Okay then, this is our plan: We will put the chains on the car tonight, Ken will get supplies from Shelly, and we leave as soon as we can in the morning. And please, no one goes anywhere alone tonight. Lucy, if you must go to the restroom, then ask Hope or Shelly to go with you, but do not go alone. These men know what we all look like, and they know that we are at this shelter."

Ken and Lucy responded in chorus, "Right."

Jay and Ken went out to the car to install the tire chains. They were looking out for anyone in the parking lot who should not be there. Seeing no one, they proceeded as planned and put the chains on the car. After they finished, Ken went and explained to Shelly that they were going to try to make it home tomorrow, so they could bring Mat's family to be with him in the hospital. He told her that they might need a few supplies just in case they ran into some trouble.

"So, can you help us out?" Ken asked.

Shelly said, "Oh, sure. I will be glad to do anything that I can do. I really thought Mat was great when he was here. I know he would love to see his family. It might even make him feel better quicker."

Shelly was so sweet and trusting that Ken hated to lie to her. But the truth just was not safe currently. To keep her from being afraid, he let her believe what she wanted to believe, and then they started off to the supply closet to make an emergency packet.

Shelly said, "Here are some sleeping bags, food, water, matches, and what about a radio? Can you use one of these?"

Ken who was glad for anything answered, "Yeah, that would be great. Shelly, um, by the way, do you happen to have any weapons around here that we could use? You know just in case we get stuck and need to scare off a bear or something."

Although Shelly was not sure that she should let him borrow the gun, she knew that the probability of encountering a wild animal was not unrealistic. Not bears of course, because they were in hibernation, but other animals were much more vicious than bears.

After weighing the possibilities, she reluctantly said, "Yes, um, I guess it would be all right to let you borrow my dad's shotgun in the back here, but only if you promise to use it in case of an extreme emergency. The bullets are back here somewhere too. Oh, here they are. Okay, you should be all set. Please let me know when you return with Mat's parents. I would really like to go to the hospital and talk with Mat, but I know I would need their permission."

Ken assured her, "Don't worry. I will come and find you first when we get back to town. You have been more than sweet to us. Thanks for helping us. We will be sure to let Mat know that you are waiting to know about his progress. Oh, and by the way, if you could keep all of this just between you and me—you know about the gun and so on—that would be best. I would not want the police to think that we are up to no good or anything. Okay?"

"Sure, no problem." Shelly let Ken know that his secret was safe with her with the signal for zipping her lips.

"Thanks, Shell. You are the greatest," Ken encouraged her.

Ken wrapped the gun in a sleeping bag so no one could see it when he went back out with the others. He picked up all the other supplies and took them to his cot. He knew that he dared not leave them in the car just in case someone snooped around tonight. At least if they were in his possession, he could keep a watch on them. He thought that he would just take them out with him in the morning.

When he got to the cot, he ran into Hope. As little girls do, she just had to ask questions.

She began by asking, "Watcha got, Ken? Can I have some? Are you going somewhere? Can I go with you? Can you help me find my mom? I know she is okay, but I need to see her and let her know that I am fine. Can you take me with you, Ken?"

Ken held up his hands and said, "Whoa, whoa, hold on, too many questions, young lady. Give me time to answer the first one before you bring on the next one. But I will try to answer the ones that I can remember. I have some supplies because we are going on a trip down the mountain to see if we can find out friend Joy and . . ."

"Joy," Hope replied with surprise. "That is my mommy's name. Maybe your friend and my mommy are the same person. Please Ken, please, pretty pleeease. Let me go with you. I need to find my mommy."

"Sweetie," Ken kindly replied so as not to let Hope down too hard, "Although you do look a lot like my Joy, I can assure you she is not your mom. She does not have any children. We thought that maybe she got lost up here somewhere, but we could not find her, so we are going to try to follow her stops back home and see what we can find. And no, I am sorry, but it is not safe for you to go with us. And besides, your mommy will more than likely come here to find you."

Hope looked intently at Ken and said, "No, my mommy can't come and find me here. She has been hurt, and she cannot get to me. I have to go to her."

As Ken stared at Hope once again with absolute astonishment, he told her, "Honey, I do not know where you get these ideas that you have been telling us, but I do know that it is not safe for you to go down the mountain with us. Besides, Shelly would not let you go anyway. She is like your big sister here. She has been watching out for you, right?"

"Yes, she has been good, but that is because she knows my father. She speaks to him every day," Hope explained to Ken.

Ken came back with, "Well, Hope, if Shelly speaks to your father every day, then why has he not come to get you yet? Is he hurt or in another country?"

Hope replied, "No it is not like that. He just wants me to find my mommy and let her know that I am okay."

Ken, realizing that he was not going to understand this little Einstein, decided to just close the subject by saying, "I am sure you know exactly what you mean, but it still does not change the fact that it is not safe for you to go with us."

Hope looked at Ken with a very serious expression and said, "Oh, Ken, if you only knew what I know, you would know that having me around is the safest way to travel." Hope then smiled and turned over and drifted sweetly off to sleep. The expression on her face was almost as if she were talking to the angels themselves.

Ken nodded his head in curiosity and said, "Okay, little lady; you are so headstrong. You and my Joy are unquestionably alike; that is for darn sure. Sleep tight, Little One. I hope you do find your mommy soon."

Just then Lucy and Jay came back to the cots where Ken and Hope were. Ken told Jay that Hope wanted to go with them and that she had her mind set that their Joy and her mommy were somehow connected. "They just happen to have the same name, so she is stuck on the idea that they might be the same person. I tried to tell her that was not possible, but she is so strong-willed. She insists on going with us, but I told her it was not safe. So, as much as I hate to do it, we are going to have to sneak out before she gets up in the morning."

Lucy said, "Oh, I hate to do that. There is something about her that reminds me of Joy. And it is funny to listen to the way she talks about things. Either she has some kind of sixth sense, or she is a little loopy. I am not quite sure which, but she cannot go with us. That would really be a bad scene."

Jay said, "Right, so we will sneak out in the morning before she gets up. Then after we get this all worked out, we will try to find her again and help her. Maybe we can run an article in the paper to help her. She really is sweet, but very strange. I am really confused about who her daddy is. Oh well, let's get some sleep. It is going to be a long day, and we will need our rest. Goodnight."

They all snuggled into their respective cots and after a while, they were able to doze off.

CHAPTER THIRTEEN
Extra Blankets

Jay was the first one to open his eyes. He stretched and looked over at Hope's bed. He looked around to see if he could see her. Suddenly, he spotted her on her way to the restroom, with her little teddy bear tucked under her arm. He quickly woke Ken and Lucy and whispered, "Hey, you guys, Hope just left to go to the restroom. If we are going to sneak out, it better be now. Come on!"

Lucy and Ken wiped the sleep from their eyes, gathered their supplies, and headed for the door. All the while they were looking over their shoulders to make sure that Hope had not spotted them. They really hated to do this, but it was just not safe on the road. They were taking a big risk, and they did not want to be responsible for risking Hope's life as well. They made it to the door and into the car. Lucy got into the back, and Ken put the box of supplies on the back seat with Lucy. He saw a large stack of blankets on the back floorboard with a note on them that read:

Dear Ken, Jay, and Lucy,

Thanks for all your help. I thought you could use a few extra blankets. Come back and see me soon, and let Mat know where I am and how I can help him.
— Shelly

"Aww, that is so sweet. We really can use them too. It is so cold out here," Ken said.

"Come on guys, we have got to go. Hope might already be looking for us," Jay reminded them.

Just as they pulled out of the parking lot, they saw a van pull up to the front door of the shelter. Out of curiosity, Lucy looked back to see who it was and to see if she saw Hope anywhere. "Oh, my goodness! You two would not believe who I just saw going into the shelter," Lucy shouted.

Jay asked, "Who, Luus?"

Lucy quickly told him, "Those four preachers. We got out just in time."

"Well, only Shelly and Hope know what we are planning to do. Shelly won't tell because I asked her not to," Ken reasoned. But then they all looked at each other and said, almost at the same time, "But Hope will."

Jay said, "Well, maybe they don't know that we were with her. Anyway, there is no turning back now. We are on our way. Does anybody know how to pray? If so, I would be using that skill right now."

Ken said, "Shelly prayed for us, and I think that means we are covered, at least for a little while. She reads her Bible all the time too. She really was sweet to help us the way she did. We have to remember to fix her up with Mat when he gets better."

Jay chimed in, "Yeah, if . . . he gets better, and from what I saw, that is a really big if."

Lucy spoke up from the back seat, "Let's change the subject. See if you can find some music. Just don't let me hear any songs like "Let It Snow." I have had enough of this stuff to last me a lifetime. After all of this, I might just take a long vacation to Florida."

All agreed and decided to put the situation out of their minds at least for right now. Ken pulled out the map that was in the glove box and started trying to figure out the best route to take. He asked Jay what he thought.

Jay responded, "Well, I think that the interstate might be the best way. Joy usually takes the most direct route anywhere. We will look that way, assuming that she is not with those four preachers. I think that after what I saw of Mat, she would have a much better chance of survival in these woods than with those four."

Ken agreed and began to map out the best way to get to the interstate. After traveling a little while, they saw some lights ahead at the entrance to the interstate.

Ken said, "Look, there has been an accident or something. Pull over; there is an officer." Jay rolled down his window and pulled up to where the officer was stopping drivers.

"What is the problem, officer?"

As the officer looked all through the car to see if there was anything wrong, he said, "A tractor-trailer has turned over further up the highway. It had some chemicals in it. This interstate has been closed until that is cleaned up. No one can pass; it might not be safe."

Ken began to plead, "But officer, we need to . . ."

Jay, worried that it might not be safe. Remembering that they had a gun in the back, Jay stopped Ken and finished his sentence for him. "We need to turn around and take the other road. We are just trying to get to a friend's house. Her mother is sick, and we are going to help her out. Thank you, officer, for your help."

The officer looked at them as if he wanted to see what they had in the back of the car with Lucy. He rubbed his chin as though he was trying to make a decision. "Well, then, be on your way," he finally said.

Jay replied, "Thank you, officer. We will take that road over there. It will be a nice change of scenery from the interstate. Thank you again." He turned the car around and headed up the long, winding road that is the only other route down the mountain.

After they are away safely, Jay chided Ken, "Are you out of your mind? We have a shotgun in the back without a permit, and we also are running from four preachers who have the law in their back pockets.

What were you thinking? I tell you what, if we get stopped again, just act like you have a sore throat and can't talk. You got me, Bud?"

Feeling convicted, Ken sheepishly said, "I'm sorry, you know me. Sometimes, I just don't think."

Jay restored him back to grace by saying, "It's all right, Bud. I am sorry, but I am just a little tense right now. I want to find Joy and get home and then get back to stop these preachers and hopefully make it back in time for Mat."

Ken said, "I know . . . me too. So, are we cool?"

Jay answered, "Yeah, you know we are."

With anticipation, they started off on the road that would take them the long way. None of them believed that Joy would have ever come this way. They all agreed that she was too much of a city girl to want to take this long way up the mountain. But they had been given no other option than this one. And they felt that they would have to work with the only option they had been granted.

They quickly got back into the routine of things and were on their way once again. As they listened to the radio, they heard a weather reporter say that it would be clear and cool and that with the worst of the storm over, things would soon be getting back to normal.

Lucy began laughing sarcastically. "Huh, I do not know if I can ever get back to normal after this. You know, it really has made me think about a few things, like what is next after this life? And how do you do it right down here so you can get the best of what's up there or out there—I am not sure. Shelly seemed to really know a lot about what was up there.

She talked a lot about God and Jesus and heaven and the Bible. She talked about Jesus as if He were her friend. I wish I had someone like that to help us out right now. Shelly also read a lot of her favorite Bible verses to me. I did not understand them all, but she did read me a story about this man and his lost son, and it really was good. It reminded me of how far apart I am from my parents and how much I have been missing them. We left on bad terms, but they are still my parents.

"But anyway, the story was about a young man whose father was rich. So, the son asked his dad to give him a lot of money so he could go and like find himself or something. His dad agreed. Then the son went and wasted all the money and found himself eating out of the same bin as the pigs—which I thought was gross and disgusting. But it was in the Bible; she showed it to me. Anyway, back to the story. After he had had enough, he thought that if he went back to his dad, at least he would get some people food to eat. He like knew that his old man would really be mad, but he did not care; he just wanted to go home."

Ken questioned, "Well, what happened when he went home? Did the Bible have all the cuss words that the old dude spouted out?"

Lucy got a faraway look as she said, "That's just it. The guy's dad did not act at all like his son thought he would. Shelly said that this story was supposed to be like a story about us and Jesus and how even if we run away, He will always take us back." Lucy stared out the window with a hopeless, homesick expression and then said, "His dad was waiting and hoping for his son to come home. The story said that when the father saw the son even way off in the distance, he started to run to him, and then he fell on his son's neck and . . ."

Just then a muffled voice was heard to say with great childlike joy, "He kissed him!" Hope popped her head out from under the supposed stack of blankets and said again, "The father ran to him and kissed him. I always love that story when my father tells it."

Jay slammed on the brakes and pulled the car off on the shoulder of the road. And he began to demand some answers, "Young lady, how did you get in here? Why have you been hiding from us?"

Hope calmly replied, "Well, I told Ken that I had to go and find my mommy, and I knew that you were all going away. I got some extra blankets and made a note and hid in the car until you got ready to go."

In utter frustration, Jay asked, "I saw you going to the restroom. How could you have done all that?"

Hope answered, "I just did."

Jay said, "All right, we cannot go back, but we cannot take you over the state line either. They will surely think we are kidnappers. And won't that be a rich irony?! We go on a mission to stop a group of bad people who hurt children, and then we get thrown into jail for stealing a child. The irony of our plight is certainly not lost on me. All right, you stay here and Lucy, Ken, and I are going to step out of the car and have a discussion about this."

They got out of the car. Jay was extremely mad; he could not believe that they had let this happen. He was pacing up and down the road, flailing his hands in a mere fit. Then he stopped dead in his tracks as he noticed that there were some marks on the road. He ran to where the marks were leading and looked over the side. Frantically, he ran back to the car and said to Ken, "What kind of car did the rental car company say that Joy rented?"

Ken replied, "A Chrysler Sebring. Why?"

Jay said, "Come here and look at this!" They all ran over and followed the path of the black marks on the road. Then they stared in amazement.

Jay was the first one to say it: "Does that look like a Chrysler Sebring to you?"

Ken said nervously, "Yes, it does."

Lucy said, "I'll go and get little Miss Stowaway from the car, and we will go check it out."

Ken answered, "Good idea. We don't want any police to stop by and start asking questions. She will get us all locked up."

Lucy hurried back to the car and opened the door on the side where Hope had popped out from the blankets, but she did not see her. She searched through the blankets one by one and called for Hope. But she could not find her. Lucy ran back toward Ken and Jay and shouted, "She is not in the car, and I can't find her. Did you see her get out?"

Jay exclaimed, "This child is going to be the death of me! When we get back, I am going to change careers to somewhere close to the loony bin so I can be nearby when I snap. Come on, maybe she is down here using the bathroom or something. She could not have gone on the other side; there is a rock wall. And even little Miss Stubborn Britches could not scale that wall. Let's get down there to that car."

CHAPTER FOURTEEN
Dear Caleb

"The soup is good; you are a good cook," Joy said as she blew on a spoonful of the steamy broth.

Caleb never responded to the compliment. Now that she was ready to go, he became very matter-of-fact.

"I think I had better go ahead and put that tire back on the truck—maybe even put some chains on the tires. Then we will be ready to leave in the morning. I can take you to the nearest phone if you like or even to the hotel or whatever you need." Caleb said all this to Joy as if he were asking for permission.

"Very well then; it is settled . . . in the morning it is. Say, what was wrong with your truck anyhow? I mean why is it still on the jack with the one tire missing?" Joy surmised that changing the subject would be more comfortable than trying to muster up a 'thank you' or even an 'I really do appreciate your help.'"

But she secretly wanted to just talk and have a deep conversation with him. She had never felt this way before. She thought maybe it was what she heard on the tape or read in the letter, but either way, she was drawn to know more about Caleb. However, she was afraid to let him in on her little secret—especially if it meant that she had to confess that she had been snooping about his place while he was out or asleep.

Caleb was just as nervous and wanted to talk too, but he was just plain scared of being rejected again. So, he continued with the frivolous chitchat by answering, "Oh, that. I had a flat the other day and thought I could just patch the tire, but it was too far gone. I ordered a new one, and it was just delivered about the time you showed up. Well, enough chitchat. I best get the truck ready." As he walked from the table to the back door, Caleb added, "I am sure that you are raring to get back to the big city as fast as you can. This simple life is probably too simple for you."

Reaching for his stocking cap and jacket, he stood at the back door and repeated an old John Wayne line, "Saddle up." Then he made his exit as they both chuckled a little bit at the joke. He reached into his pocket to pull out his gloves to prepare for the work that lay ahead of him.

The cold immediately whipped through the hall and into the kitchen, and like a demon snake, it coiled around Joy's legs and feet. She listened to the crunching of snow as Caleb made his way to the old truck in the driveway.

Then she got up from the table to peer out the back window, watching as Caleb began working with the jack to ensure it was still sturdy after all the snow. She noticed how strong and able he was to take care of whatever needed to be taken care of. But then she remembered that he had been incredibly tender and gentlemanly with her. He had prepared all her meals and made sure she had wood burning in the fire to keep her warm. As she watched Caleb work on that truck, she thought for just a moment about how she and that truck had something in common.

They both needed Caleb to help them get around again. For this she was thankful. But this gratitude she was feeling in her heart made her feel worse about what she was about to do by reading the letter she had found. The tape was one thing because it was not private, but this was a letter just for him. She thought to herself that if she had taken this out of a mailbox and then opened it and read it, she would have been committing a federal crime. But she had to know; she simply couldn't stand not knowing any longer. She must understand why Caleb had been scarred so badly, and she thought that this letter might make a reference to what had happened.

She took a deep breath and sat on the couch. She sat there for a moment hesitating, but then she reached into her shirt pocket and pulled the letter out. The envelopes were tinged with a little yellow around the ends. The seal had evidently been ripped open as it was jagged around the edges. The return address simply read, "Elizabeth Sanders, Chicago." As she removed the letter from inside its secure covering, she noticed two thin pages with writing on the front sides of both. She looked at the signature on the second page, and there it was. It was signed, "Your loving and grateful sister."

She became very excited, for she knew that she probably held in her hand the one piece of evidence that could open a window into Caleb and his life and those scars that he wore. She turned back to the front page and began to read:

Dear Caleb,

It was so good to see you at father's funeral. I know it must have been hard for you to come. The cancer was very difficult and painful. He was the same right up to his death. The doctors said that all the years of heavy drinking had finally taken their toll on his liver. I wish I could say he asked for forgiveness, but he never did. I wish I could say he asked about you also, but he never once did. He died just like he lived: mean, cursing, and insolent to everyone around.

Strange isn't it, Caleb? Everyone thinks they will be able to make things right on their deathbed, but human nature is such that the principles we live by are so hammered in our souls that we end up dying by the same principles, whether good or bad. The last hour was extremely difficult. He was heavily sedated for the pain and was in and out of consciousness. He would scream out sometimes and cry out that he was being tormented in some sort of flame. He spoke a few names that he must have either been remembering or was actually seeing them. I only knew a few of the names. They were some of his old drinking buddies. The strange thing is the ones he mentioned had already died. I have often wondered if he was seeing the gates of hell opening for him and recognizing some of its captives.

I am not like you, Caleb. I do not have faith. Still, I wonder at times. I write this to tell you about father and to tell you it is over. You can put him behind you now if that is possible. I will always be grateful for how you protected me from him. I know you carry the marks on your body for that protection and love for me. I know I would not be who I am today if not for you. I also know that you have suffered more than I have and even more than mother did before she died five years ago. I am so sorry to hear about your wife leaving you and about you losing your church. I am comforted by the fact that you are a man of faith even though I cannot say that I am a woman of faith.

Jerry and I and the kids are doing okay. I still see a counselor once a week. I think it is helping, but sometimes I wonder. I still have panic attacks and am still on medication. Other than that, we are fine. Caleb, I know you will be okay too. I want so much for you to be happy. When I think of what father did to all of us and what he left in his wake, I think about your strength, your courage, and your faith. Please do not lose those qualities.

Well, I need to go. Jerry and I are going away for a few days. Just know I love you and will always be grateful. Ben and Susan say hello, and Jerry wants me to tell you to come to see us anytime you want. We are your family, and we love you, Caleb.

Your loving and grateful sister, Elizabeth

Joy's hands fell to her lap still holding the thin pages. Her mind raced with all kinds of thoughts. She wanted more than ever now to know who

Caleb really was. She knew one thing now. She knew where the scars came from. Not able to read the other letter, she placed them together and back in her pocket. She felt as if she had to get up and move around. The vision of all the pain that Caleb had endured as a young child and even into his adult life was overwhelming to Joy. She walked once again to the window at the back of the cabin where she could see Caleb working. He was working so hard to get the truck ready for her, and it was cold, and she found herself aching for him.

She remembered back to when Caleb had said he believed that all things work together for good when God is in control, even the bad. At the time she first heard him say it, she thought he was a fool and that he had probably never seen real heartache to believe that. She knew that she had selfishly thought at that time, that if he had ever felt her pain, he could never say that all things work together, even the bad. But now, she was ashamed that she had ever even entertained the thought that he was a fool and had not known pain; for clearly the man knew what real suffering was. Yet he still believed. She began to cry for Caleb and his loss and what he had gone through. And she felt mortified that she had treated him the way she had and that he had still been so nice to her. For the first time, as she looked at him, she saw Caleb, the man, not the man with all the scars. She could see his face while he was outside, and she smiled as she thought that his scars looked more like badges of courage to her now. She just stood there daydreaming as she looked out the window and thought about all that she had just read.

Suddenly, Joy noticed her. Down at the bend in the driveway, a little girl. A little blonde-haired girl! This was no vision. She could see her. She just stood there as if she were waiting to be seen. Then suddenly, she ran around the bend and disappeared down the drive. Forgetting to get any extra clothing or coat, Joy dashed through the back door screaming, "Did you see her?"

Caleb was huddled down under the truck with a chain in his hand and was startled, to say the least. He dropped the chains and stood up to see what in the world was the matter. He thought that Joy must have seen someone behind him that meant to do him harm. So, he looked around behind him to see what he could see, but he saw nothing. He just saw Joy running toward him with no coat or hat on.

"What? What is wrong?" Caleb quickly responded looking around again to see what Joy must have been talking about.

"Did you see her? The little girl, Caleb. It was the little girl I told you about."

"I do not know what you are talking about," Caleb said.

Joy's anxiety was contagious, and Caleb rushed over to her. Without even noticing, he placed his hands on her shoulders. This was only the second time he had reached out to touch her, the first being when he had to look at her ankle to see if it was broken.

"I think it was her! It looked just like her!" Joy kept exclaiming.

"Calm down, Joy. Get a hold of yourself and tell me what is wrong. Who do you think you saw?" Caleb anxiously asked, holding Joy in front of him as if he needed to see her lips move to understand what she was saying.

Joy began to try to explain, but she was very frantic, "The little girl. The little blonde! Remember, I told you I was sure that I had seen a little girl in the road. It was seeing her that caused me to begin to lose control of the car. I think, no, I know I just saw her again! She was standing down there at the bend in the drive. When I noticed her, she just ran down the road. We have got to go and get her. I do not know how she could have survived out here all his time and through that storm. She might be hurt or scared. Please, please Caleb, we have to go now and find her! I let one child be lost from me, and I promised that I would never do that again. Please, we must go now!"

Caleb looked at Joy deeply moved by what she had just said, and he was stunned. He thought maybe she had a fever or something, but she just kept pointing toward the direction that they needed to go. Still, Caleb could not see anyone or anything.

"Joy, you have got to go inside; it is freezing out here," Caleb insisted.

Joy had hardly noticed that she was shivering. Caleb wrapped his coat around her and pressed his arms around her as he walked her toward the porch.

"We've got to get to her now," Joy blurted sternly.

Before Caleb knew what to say, he found himself lying, "Okay, okay, we will go and look for her. But first, you need to get better dressed for the drive. This old truck doesn't have good heat, and I have only put chains on the back tires, but if you insist, we will go."

Once inside Joy hurried to the window in the kitchen to see if she could spot the little girl from that side of the house. But she saw nothing.

Caleb busied himself looking for an old jacket and a warm hat that Joy could make do with.

"Go and put some extra socks on your feet," Caleb said as he placed the jacket around Joy as if she were a child going off to school. "Here is a hat. Put it on and pull it down over your ears," Caleb told her in a commanding voice that suddenly was out of character for him.

After Joy suited up, they hurried out to the truck and jumped in the old cab. The hinges made an awful squeaking noise as they shut the doors behind them. Caleb turned the key that was always left in the ignition. Slowly the truck's engine turned over with a loud backfire. He pumped the gas pedal a couple of times as if to say, "Come on girl, I'm counting on you." Caleb then spun the back tires as he headed the truck out and quickly turned the big steering wheel as if he were spinning a large submarine around. The engine raced as the truck pulled out of the snow that still covered the ground. Once he steered the truck onto the drive, the tires caught better traction, and around the bend they went. After they cleared the bend, Caleb slowed up just a little and rolled down his window a bit.

"What are you doing?" Joy asked. But there was only silence. Caleb kept a steady but slow pace as he craned his neck out the window, moving his head to the left and then to the right.

"What are you looking for?" Joy insisted that he answer her. She thought they should be moving forward faster than they were. She was becoming quite impatient with Caleb by this time.

"I am looking for footprints," Caleb replied defensively. "But I don't see any so far. She might not stick to the drive. If she is scared or lost, she might be in these woods, and it would be very hard to spot her from the road."

Just then, Joy shouted loudly and with great agitation as she pointed down the drive where it sloped toward the next road, "Look! There she is! Do you see her?"

"Oh my, I do see her!" Caleb expressed with a bewildered tone. He had thought for sure that Joy could not have possibly seen a little girl out in these woods in this cold. But she was so agitated and insistent that they go as fast as possible that Caleb really had no choice but to humor her. But now he could see the little girl too, and he was shocked, to say the least.

Coming down the mountain, the truck rattled, and the springs screeched telling its age. Then just as before, the child was out of sight. It was as if the small youngster were baiting them to follow. Still moving forward, Caleb pressed down on the gas and rolled up the window with a hurried fury. The road that sloped downward was about two miles long. It was still very slick as the sun was unable to penetrate through the thick trees. However, once they reached the bottom of that treacherous road, there was another road that was safer to navigate.

Joy looked around and noticed that this new road was the one where she had her accident. She knew that her car must be close. She was suddenly, thrown back into the initial fear that she had felt when she first awakened after her car ran off the road. She could not believe how much had happened in such a short time. And how much Caleb had been her saving grace. As she looked at the surrounding area, she could see that she was indeed very lucky to have found Caleb. Due to her state of shock after the accident, Joy had not noticed how truly isolated she had been. But now, her eyes were suddenly opened to the real danger she was in that day, especially considering the storm that hit after she found Caleb. This realization caused Joy to shudder at the thought of what could have happened had she not kept moving in search of help. She did not know whether to sink into fear of the what-ifs or to stand and count her blessings.

Just then, she was drawn back into the present when she spotted the little girl again. And she heard Caleb shout, "Look, there she is again!"

As before, the child suddenly seemed to move into a stealth zone and was not visible. As they reached the bottom of the road, the truck came to an abrupt stop. Both Joy and Caleb looked north and south for any sign of the small child or any evidence of where she might have been or where she might be.

"There she is . . . down there," Joy cried as she nudged Caleb on his arm. Turning right, Caleb entered the road. Joy had not realized that they were headed back to where her car sat in the ditch. Up ahead another car became visible as it was parked on the side of the road. Suddenly, Joy grasped that they were coming up to the place where her car was wrecked.

"Who are those people?" Caleb asked, thinking to himself that he had not seen them and that they were parked in a very dangerous spot on the road. He seemed annoyed with them at that moment.

Joy's eyes widened and then a knowing smile suddenly ran across her face. "I don't believe it," Joy said rather slowly and with utter amazement. "It is my crew. My crew? I cannot believe it!" she said with glee in her voice.

Caleb, not knowing exactly what she meant, pulled up behind the car. Joy quickly opened the door of the truck and almost jumped out before Caleb came to a complete stop. As Joy threw herself out of the truck, she started running toward her crew. Her emotions overflowed as she began to cry tears of release. Running as well as she could, she locked arms with her crew members. They were as stunned as she was. At first, silent amazement filled the air. Joy, forgetting about the little girl for a moment, began to spill over with excitement—talking so fast that no one could understand what she was talking about.

Ken was the first of the crew members to speak. He was more than overjoyed to see her. He had been so worried about her and thought of how his life would be if she were not around. He had secretly purchased a new porcelain doll for when they found Joy. The doll had long blonde hair and a pink dress and rosy cheeks. He ran to the car to get the doll, and as he did, he said, "Joy I am so happy to see that you are all right. I have been saving something for you. Hold on." He then brought her the doll wrapped in pink tissue and pink ribbons. He slowly handed it to Joy as he gave her a welcome back hug. He said, "We saw your car, and we became even more worried because of the looks of it. How are you doing?"

Joy began to tell them some of the details of her accident. "I decided at the last moment to take the long way to Asheville, so I could take in some sights. After my wreck, I was hurt, and I did not know what to do. My cell phone was broken into several pieces; I had no way of getting help. So, after I spent one night passed out on the ground, I was able to put together a crutch and make it to where I found Caleb. He is the one who took care of me and made sure that I lived through that terrible storm. If it had not been for him . . ."

Jay broke in as she told her story, "Who is Caleb?"

Looking around for him, Joy noticed that he had stayed behind in the truck. Motioning with her hand as if she were directing traffic, Joy signaled for Caleb to get out of the truck and come and meet everyone.

Caleb shut off the truck and came reluctantly to join the reunion. Joy introduced everyone and began to explain to Caleb that these people were like family to her. "They are the crew that I have been talking about. And look, Ken has even brought me a welcome-back present. I cannot wait to see what it is. Ken is always so thoughtful, and he knows what everyone likes."

With tears filling her eyes, Joy began to open the special gift that her friend had brought her as everyone else stood around her. As she opened it, she remembered how she and Caleb had come to be here in the first place, and she looked at the doll and said, "This looks like her! Have you seen her? She is a little blonde-haired girl, and she helped us to find you."

Lucy said with great shock, "What? We also had a little blonde-haired girl with us who caused us to stop at this very place where we found your car. Her name is Hope. But she cannot be the same child. The child with us came from Asheville. She hid in our car, and we did not know it until we got near here."

Jay added, "We are looking for our little one too. She was with us in the car, but we have been unable to find her for the last half hour. We thought that maybe she had gone down this way to use the bathroom, but we are thinking that she might have gotten lost. Or knowing her, she has made friends with the little girl you are looking for, and the two of them are having a pretend tea party with the squirrels."

Abruptly, Hope came from around the back of the car. The crew all went up to her in a frenzied hurry. Joy and Caleb just stood there with their mouths wide open.

"Hope, where did you go?" Lucy asked as if she were scolding Hope for worrying everyone. Hope said nothing while she made eye contact with Joy. Joy felt as if she knew this little one. Joy walked slowly toward Hope. Locking eyes with Hope, Joy bent down in front of her and asked, "It was you up on the hillside, wasn't it? You were getting us to follow your down."

Then Joy realized that Hope had somehow brought her back together with her crew. "But how?" she asked. There is no way you could have known where I was or even who I was."

But Hope never answered her. She just stood there staring at Joy. It was the kind of look that two people exchange when they expect never to see one another again.

"Thank you," Joy expressed to Hope. "Thank you, Little One, for bringing us together again."

The crew all looked at each other with looks of puzzlement mixed with astonishment. They all wondered to themselves if Joy knew this little Hope. And if she did, how could she? Something very strange was taking place right in front of their eyes. It was as if time stood still for just a moment.

Hope looked at Joy and tenderly touched her hair and said, "You are so pretty. I knew you would be. Your face reminds me of the brightness of a sunflower. Please remember that I said you look like a sunflower every time you feel discouraged or lonely. Everything is going to be fine. My

Father sent me to tell you that He knows it was not your choice. You can let go now."

Joy was overwhelmed with surprise, and she really was afraid to think what this child might truly mean and who she might be. Joy just stared at her for a while in stunned silence. It was as if they were the only two people in the world at that moment.

Jay broke the silence by making a disclaimer, "Joy, don't think about it too hard. Hope has been saying things that we do not understand either. We call her our little Psychic. You will drive yourself crazy if you try too hard to make sense of what she says. Just say, 'All right.'"

But Joy sensed that she did understand and began to cry. It was the kind of crying that she should have been set free from a long time ago—the kind of deep crying that cleanses you to your very soul. She felt almost relieved at the words of this little one. She did not know if she was real or what, but she did know that she needed to hear what Hope had just said to her, and she had needed to hear it for a long time.

Hope's eyes were filled with tears of compassion as well, and the two of them began to cry together. Hope took Joy by the hand and led her away from everyone else so they could talk alone. The others just stood watching as Joy and Hope walked away hand in hand.

Joy turned to the others and said, "Wait by the car, and I will be back in a minute." Then Joy and Hope continued until they were out of the sight of the others.

Hope found a stump for Joy to sit on and rest for a while. Then Hope began to wipe away the tears on Joy's face. She then softly said, "Don't cry. . . Mommy."

Joy looked at her and looked at her again, and then she could see it. She was the age that she would have been if she had been allowed to live. Joy was overwhelmed with shame and said, "How could this be? How can you be here? What is this all about? This cannot be possible. Did I die in the crash, and is this the way I am to be punished forever? What is going on?"

Hope began to explain, "This is real, Mommy, and I do not want you to worry about me anymore. I have been very happy with my Father in heaven, and He sent me because He knows that you are using your pain about me to hurt some of His servants. Sure, some of the ones you have stopped were of their father the devil, but the ones that you are after now are really of God. They have been praying for you for a long time. The four preachers that you set out to expose cannot be exposed for anything but good works. They really are at heart all that they claim to be. That is the main reason God sent me. He knew that I could be the one to reach you when no one else could even get close to you.

Everything that you have been going through was all God's divine plan. I was there at the wreck. Something had to come into your life that would get you to sit silently and listen to the still, small voice of the Holy Spirit. And just like you and the way you always get the story behind the story, God is the beginning and the end. He is and knows the whole story all the time. This is why you and Caleb were brought together. He is also precious to God, and he has been hurt so terribly that he too has found it hard to let others know him in his entire God-given beauty. But Mommy, you have been able to see it, haven't you?"

Joy said, "Yes, I have; he is a good man, and I have been humbled by the sacrifice he made for his sister and her safety."

Hope reassured Joy by saying, "God is working in his life as well. Just let God do what He does best. I like to call Him the Master of the Surprise."

Joy asked Hope, "But what do I do now? How do I explain this? They will surely lock me up for being crazy."

"Mommy," Hope said, "You need to pray and ask Jesus to come into your heart and save your soul, and then He will do the rest. You have something very hard that you are going to have to do very soon but know that I will be there too."

Joy knew that she needed to pray. She was so tired of being angry and running. She wanted to be done with the past and move on to the future. In utter humility, Joy bowed her head and took Hope's hand, and said, "Father, you know all that I have done and that I do not deserve to have the blessing of this child standing in my presence right now. This can only be a miracle that you have granted to me because you do love me. I am sorry that I have caused so much harm to you over the years—not to mention the harm I have done to myself as well. Thank you for forgiving me and thank you for working this out all for my good. Help me to serve you and love you and help those around me to know you too. Amen." Joy lifted her eyes and saw Hope standing in front of her. She had a particular flow about her that had not been there before.

Hope then said, "Mommy, you cannot tell everyone else who I really am. I will let you tell Caleb because he needs to be set free too. God has great things yet for him to do, and you are going to be instrumental in helping Caleb get to the point of using his scars for the good of God's kingdom. What he did for his sister needs to be shared with others who are hurting. You and he together can be used to help mend the scars, inner and outer, of many who are hurting in this world. But for now, we will need to go back to Asheville and see Mat. He is in the hospital there. And God will help you to know what do to after that."

Joy agreed and gave her little girl a hug that she had always dreamed of giving her. Then Joy looked at Hope and put in her hand the beautiful Porcelain doll that Ken had just given her and said with tears in her eyes, "This is for all the dolls that I should have been able to give you, my precious one."

Hope said, "Oh, Mommy, thank you so much, I think I am going to call her . . . Angel."

Hope and Joy just stood there looking at each other, knowing that Joy had become a Christian and that one day, the two of them will get to spend eternity in heaven together. Joy did not want this time with Hope to end. Finally, she felt so loved, so accepted for who she truly is, and she had never known this feeling so completely before. But they both knew that others were waiting in the cold for them to come back and explain. After one last hug, they slowly walked back to where everyone else was waiting.

Without giving anyone a chance to ask probing questions that she preferred to avoid, Joy said, "We need to go see Mat; I am going to ride with Caleb. I need to talk to him about a few things that I have on my mind."

Hope, cradling her new baby doll, reacted the same way and said, "I will ride back with Lucy, Ken, and Jay."

And even though everyone else wanted to ask what had just happened between those two, no one was brave enough to make the first move. They all wanted to know who this Hope was, how she knew Joy, and how the same child could bring them all together. Talk about confusion. They were in a state of complete confusion—except for Joy and Hope who looked like they had everything in life figured out and that no problem was too big for them to conquer together. So, the crew just stuck with the plan that Joy and Hope had announced, and back to Asheville, they went.

CHAPTER FIFTEEN
Confession

There was silence in the truck between Caleb and Joy for a long time. Caleb did not know what in the world had just happened, but he could definitely see a difference in Joy's countenance. He was afraid to ask because he was not sure he wanted to know. It might require him to come out of his protective and secluded world of the cabin in the woods, and he was not sure that he was ready to put himself out there again. The stares and comments about his scars were still painful—especially because he received these scars because of his deep love for his sister. When the jokes and jeers came, he just wished that he could be totally free of his scars, emancipated from them as it were. As a young man in college, he studied what the word *emancipated* meant; it meant to be free of or liberated from. This sounded like heaven to him, but then he would be faced with the stares of another person who was seeing him for the first time. The eyes of those individuals were always like mirrors for Caleb and reflected how he really looked to everyone. So, he just decided to play it safe and help Joy get to Asheville, and then he thought that he would just go back into hiding in the cabin. He knew that he would miss Joy, but he never imagined that she would miss him. This was all fine to him, he thought, "I really do not need anyone in my life."

But while riding toward Asheville, Joy took a deep breath and turned to Caleb. She blurted out as if to cleanse herself of hidden sins, "Caleb, I looked in your trunk and I listened to your tape about the fundamentals of the gospel. There, I said it. I admit it, and I hope you can forgive me. I was only curious to find out about you and what happened to you. And since you would not tell me, I let myself find out via snooping. Can you ever forgive me?"

Caleb just sat there a minute as if he were loading up to really let loose on her. But then he said with a slight grin on his face, "Do you think you were the only one snooping around? I knew all along you were spying on me. I even planted the tape player where you could find it, and then I left you alone so you could listen to the tape. I really wanted to talk to you so many times, I mean really talk to you, but you seemed to go crazy when I mentioned anything about God, so I just let you alone."

Joy began to laugh and said, "So the queen of snoop has been out-snooped." She then nudged Caleb with a gleeful jolt. For the first time, there was no awkwardness between them. They were like best friends, laughing and joking with one another.

Caleb began to think that there really was something very different about Joy, but he could not put his finger on it. He decided to satisfy his curiosity by asking her what she thought about the tape. "So, what did you think about what you heard? Do you still think I am a crazy mountain man?" He was joking, but at the same time, he was truly afraid that Joy might use that sharp, two-edged sword she called a tongue to mess up the mood that they had going. But he was willing to risk it this time, so he squared his mental feet, as it were, and waited for the expected tongue-lashing to commence.

There was silence for a moment and neither Joy nor Caleb expected what came next. Joy became very serious for a moment. She turned and looked directly at Caleb and said more sincerely and more genuinely than she had ever said anything in her life, "The truth is Caleb, I think you are the most beautiful person I have ever known, and I want to know more about you. The words that you spoke of on the tape really reached me.

I did not know that God's Word could be made to be so real. And the sacrifices you made for your sister . . ."

Caleb changed his tone as he asked, "And how do you know about that? That is private and very painful, and we do not know each other that well. I do not appreciate that you delved further than I had planned for you too."

Joy sensed that this was a very scary area for Caleb and began to reassure him by saying, "Caleb, I know that you have been very hurt in your life, and so have I. You once told me that God works out everything, even the bad, for our good. Maybe that is why we found each other. Maybe we are supposed to help each other get over the hurt enough to go on to help others. But we are not to forget the hurt so that we become calloused. To me, each one of your scars is like a medal of honor that says you loved so much that you even gave of your own flesh. Every scar that you have is a reminder that you set someone else free. And I know that your sister feels liberated because of what you bore for her. And what you did for her is exactly what Jesus did for us. He loved us so much that He gave His own life so that we could be safe. Caleb, in God's eyes, and to me, you are a walking testimony of His sacrifice for us. God wants you to use your scars for His glory, not to hide them. There are so many people in this world who have been hurt, but because their pain is on the inside, they never take the chance to share with others how God can use even the bad for our good. I once heard someone very special to me call Him the 'Master of the Surprise.'

We can only see things while we are in the midst of the mess, but God sees the entire situation from the beginning to the end. He knows that if we let him have control, our lives can be blessings, despite the hardships that are brought on us by others or ourselves. That is how I see you, Caleb, as a blessing forged in the face of the hardships in which you had no fault. I know you believe this deep in your heart because you are the one who told me first. I must admit that when I heard you say that all things—even the bad—work for the good of those who love God, I thought surely you were delusional or crazy. But now I see it, and I not only believe it, but I know that God is in the business of setting us free. I will never forget this day and this entire experience and how He has truly set me free today."

Caleb began to cry. He too needed to just let out the pain that he had been hiding. He had never in his life felt the way he did right then. He could not believe that this was the same person who had stayed with him in his cabin for the past few days. So, he asked her, "Where is all this coming from? How could you be so different so fast? What has happened to you?"

Joy smiled and looked out the window and said, "Oh, you could just say I have a little angel watching over me."

Caleb did not know what she was talking about, but he could see that there was something very different about her. He was more drawn to her at this moment than he had ever been drawn to anyone else in his life. And he strongly felt the need to tell her everything that had ever happened to him. He longed to hear all her stories too.

He reached over and took her hand and said, "Well, since you want to know what happened to me so badly, I will tell you. My name is Caleb Nobah Sims; my name means "barking dog." I was given this name because my mother could not stand to hear a child cry. She really hated children altogether actually. My father was a terrible and mean alcoholic, and my sister and I spent most of our lives either hiding or running from him. Even with all the scars that I have, I still know that these are nothing compared to what he would have done if he had been able to catch us when he was at his drunkest. My sister and I learned very early to read the signs of when he would be the most dangerous. But sometimes he would surprise us, and he would always start with my baby sister. I could not stand to see her get hit; she was so small, so frail. If he had been allowed to do to her what he had done to me, there is no way that she could have lived. And one thing that was the worst was that he never even acted like he was sorry after he sobered up. Most drunks are at least remorseful in some way after they come to their senses. But not my dad. He was mean and cruel all the time."

He kept right on pouring out his heart to Joy, explaining everything she had wanted to know. She hung on to every word. Every aspect of his life fascinated her, and she felt so comfortable with him.

And Caleb felt like he finally had a friend who did not just see him as a man full of scars but just as a man. This acceptance opened both Joy and Caleb to help each other to continue the healing that God had begun in them.

"Well, Joy, now you know a lot more about me, but what about you. What is your story?" Caleb inquired of Joy.

Joy felt just as comfortable with telling Caleb everything as she had ever felt in her life. She had never felt this free before. She had always tried to keep these memories down where no one could see them. She even feared that somehow, they would destroy her sanity one day. But with the way Caleb had unlocked his heart to her, she wanted to let him help her bear the burdens that had been weighing her down all these years.

Joy opened her mouth to speak words that had never been spoken of before by saying, "My dad was good when I was small, but he was very strict. He was a leader in our church, and he felt he had to keep up appearances at church. So, at home we lived one way; with the church people, we lived another. But when I was a junior in high school, I made a terrible mistake the night of my prom, and I became pregnant."

Joy began to cry so hard that she could not speak. Caleb did not know what to do. He thought maybe he had upset her. He tenderly pushed her hair back from her face and said, "Joy, what is it? What is wrong?"

Joy was very ashamed of what she had to say next, but she wanted to be liberated from this. To overcome her great trepidation and trembling, she took a deep cleansing breath and said, "Oh Caleb, please do not judge me for what I must tell you next. My father was so upset and worried that my child and I would be a disgrace to him because of his standing at church, that he made my mother take me to get . . . an . . . abortion." She felt as if the weight of all her troubles and fears had suddenly been lifted from her. She was afraid of what Caleb would say next. But she knew she wanted him to say something.

"Joy." Caleb looked at her with eyes full of compassion and kindness that she had never seen in another man before and said, "Remember that God uses all things for the good. Even those things that we are so ashamed of that we dare not share them with others. I want to thank you for sharing this with me. I know God understands and has forgiven you. Tell me about your child. Did you know what sex it was? Did you give it a name?"

That is when Joy looked at Caleb and smiled as she said, "I knew she was a little girl, but I did not know her name until tonight. Her name is Hope."

Caleb almost ran the truck off the road, so he pulled over before he asked the next question: "Joy, what do you mean that you did not know her name until tonight? What are you telling me?"

Joy continued, "Hope is her name. I know that this is going to be hard for you to believe, but when that little blonde girl named Hope took me off to talk to me, she had a message for me and for you too. She said that she was my baby; she even called me Mommy." Joy then heard the name as it rang back into her ear. "Oh Caleb, she called me Mommy. I still can't believe it. She said that God the Father had sent her to set me free from the pain of the abortion, and He knew that I needed to see her for me to believe it. It was so unreal. But at the same time, I knew who she was when I really looked at her.

You see, I have been punishing God's people for a long time for what my earthly father did to me. I was even on a mission to destroy the lives of four very good servants of God at the time that I saw Hope on the road and had the accident. God masterminded the entire situation. I was supposed to find you and tell you, and we were both to be set free of the scars that have been keeping us from being useful to Him. Yes, we both have scars. Mine are just as visible to the heart of God as yours are to you when you look in the mirror. Our scars were not as He intended, but He can use them for His glory. I still cannot believe it. My head and my heart are still reeling at what I have seen and felt today. I know that I will never again look at life or people the same. I am so humbled that God would care enough about me to go to all this trouble—just so I could come to

Him. And Caleb, that is just what I did when I went with Hope. I asked Jesus to come into my heart and set me free for the first time in my life. Right now, I am not only free of the past, but I am free for the present and for the future. I am completely free!"

Caleb was speechless and did not know what to say. He too had seen the little girl and the way she led them to the road where Joy's crew was standing. And he could not deny that Hope and Joy looked exactly alike. He also could sense that there was something different about Joy after her encounter with this child. They were both overwhelmed with happiness and amazement, and they sat together in silence for a while taking it all in.

Slowly, Caleb began the journey once again toward the hospital where Mat was. He did not know Mat, but he did not want to let Joy get away from him. Also, he did not want her to feel like he was rejecting her after all she had told him. They looked at each other and smiled a thankful smile as they enjoyed the drive together and pondered what they had just shared with one another.

It seemed that time flew by, and they soon found themselves at the hospital where Mat was. They parked and got out of the vehicles and met in the front entryway.

Jay said, "Let me warn you, he looks beyond what you could imagine, and you will be shocked. I signed a paper so that no one could see him except us. So be on the lookout for anyone else if you know what I mean."

The sliding door opened into a waiting room, and there in the corner were the four preachers holding hands and praying. They seemed to be deep in prayer for someone. There was an awesome respectful silence from the others in the waiting room for these four men and what they were doing.

But Jay became enraged and started to go over to them as if he were going to take them out of this world. He was still under the impression that they had hurt his friend and the children. Joy had not yet told him and the rest of the crew that there was no story about these men. But she did know that God would take care of this situation somehow.

Just then Hope, with her little precious doll in one hand, took Jay's hand with her other hand and said, "Jay, it is okay; you wait right here."

Jay did not know why, but he stopped in his tracks and watched as Hope went over and took the hands of the ministers as they prayed. Rubbing his eyes in disbelief, Jay thought he caught a glimpse of light encircling all of them, but then it was gone. Yet Jay was calm even though he did not know what was going on.

Joy looked at Jay, Ken, and Lucy and said, "Don't worry. I have done some research, and there is no story here. These are not bad men as we thought; rather, they are who they claim to be. They are for real. I am only sorry that I went so far in my hunt to destroy them when they had done nothing wrong."

Jay, Lucy, and Ken were in shock that Joy would ever just back out of a story like this. Jay asked, "But what about Mat?"

Joy said, "We need to go and see him, and then we will know about Mat."

Jay led Lucy, Ken, Caleb, and Joy to Mat's room. He was there just like he was when Jay left him. The nurse said that he was having trouble breathing and that pneumonia had set in. She said that she did not know if he was going to make it.

The nurse began to explain, "Remember that the hearing is the last thing to go, so try to talk to your friend."

They encircled Mat, and Jay said, "Hey, Buddy, we found Joy. She is fine. She just had a car wreck, but Caleb here helped her stay safe until the storm passed by. We want to get you home, so can you hang on?"

Just then Mat opened his eyes and saw his friends standing there. With a faint voice that held almost no breath support at all, he whispered, "The . . . preachers . . . did . . . try . . . to . . . help . . . me. They also . . . told me . . . about Jesus . . . and heaven. I am . . . going there . . . soon."

Lucy, Ken, and Jay looked at each other and did not know what in the world he was talking about. But Joy and Caleb looked at each other as if knowing what the other one was thinking.

ACKNOWLEDGEMENTS

First and foremost, we thank God for all His love for us in the good times and the hard times of our journey. He has always guided us with His strong right hand.

We also thank Ross and Dana for prompting us to consider publishing this story, and we thank everyone who read the rough drafts and encouraged us along the way. They loved us enough to not point out all our mistakes before the editing process began. If they had not, the book may have ended up back in the trunk.

We thank Aarica for her never-ending encouragement and creative ideas, and we also thank our web team at Townsquare Interactive for their marketing and promotion of this book. We also acknowledge our wonderful staff at Beautifully Broken Counseling—especially Charlene who created the word processing document from the hard copy that had been kept in the trunk.

Finally, we thank the staff at Lucid Books for their professionalism and for taking the time to get to know our hearts as we work together to publish this book. They have been amazing in every way, and we hope to work with them again on future projects.

CPSIA information can be obtained
at www.ICGtesting.com
Printed in the USA
BVHW052354060223
658028BV00011B/434

Jay turned to the nurse and angrily said, "I told you that no one could see him except those I approve. Why is he talking about those four men? They could have done something more to hurt him. Of course, they do not want any witnesses left. This hospital is going to hear from . . ."

Just then the nurse said, "Look at his finger; he is trying to say something to you."

Jay turned to Mat and asked, "What is it, Buddy? What are you trying to say to me? Did they hurt you in any way? Remember, once for yes and twice for no."

All eyes were on Mat's hand as he slowly, but most decidedly tapped two times on the bed for no."

And then he slowly took in a great breath, exhaled a raspy rattle of a tone that is a heart-wrenching sound to hear . . . and he went limp.

The nurse said with great sadness, "I am sorry, but your friend is dead."

Everyone in the room began to feel the brunt of what had just happened. They could not believe that their friend was gone. He was so full of life, and he loved taking pictures of everything that he saw.

Just then, the nurse said, "He had some pictures on him when he came in. I knew that they might be special to his family—especially if he did not make it. I kept them here with me so they would not be lost in records." She handed the package of pictures to Joy because she was standing closest to her.

Joy took the pictures, opened the packet, and began looking at them. One by one, she passed them to the next person, so they could all look at them. There was a picture of Shelly and her warm and inviting smile. Next was a photo of Mat reading to a group of children at the shelter. The picture looked like it was taken by one of the little ones because in the top corner you could make out the image of a small finger that had slipped into the range of the eye of the camera. There was a picture of Jay hovering over a desk with his head buried in a checkbook and a picture of Ken as he was giving a gift to one of the children at the shelter. Then she saw a picture of Lucy as she made funny faces for a group of children at the shelter.

And finally, there was a picture that Joy stared at and could not believe her eyes. As the others occupied themselves looking at the other photos, Joy took a close look at this one. It was a picture of Mat as he lay in the snow at the bottom of the cliff. He was badly broken and bloody and bruised, and it pained her to see her friend in such dire straits. It appeared that he had taken it himself while he was lying in the snow waiting for help. Then upon further inspection, she saw something else in the picture. It was faded, but it was still there. Joy held the picture up to the light so she could get a closer look, and then she began to cry silently. In that picture, she saw a young girl with blonde hair. She was sitting in the snow with Mat, and it looked like she was showing him something that she had in her hand. Joy blinked once more and as the tears slowed enough for her to see clearly once again, she could see that the little blonde-haired girl was Hope. The thing she was showing Mat was her little doll named Angel that Joy had just given to Hope an hour or so ago. Joy rejoiced in her heart because once again she could see how all things work together for the good and that nothing is impossible with God.

Then she spotted something out the window that caught her attention. She went over and stood by the window and just watched, and she could see Hope take the hand of her now-departed friend Mat. Joy stood motionless and barely breathing as she watched Mat and Hope, holding her doll, walk up toward a beautiful stairway that led up into the clouds. Joy lingered a little longer there and waved, thinking of how grateful she was to finally be truly free. She knew that all this meant that Mat had also been set free.

Joy began to smile and felt so privileged and blessed because for that one still breathless moment she could see heaven accessible to her own eyes. She watched sorrowfully but hopefully as her friend and her baby girl, her doll in hand, walked into heaven together. And for the first time, she knew that she could really HOPE in ALL things.

EPILOGUE

> And we know that in all things God works for good of those who love him, who have been called according to his purpose.
> —Romans 8:28

After experiencing such a miracle and realizing that heaven is real, Joy and Caleb threw off all restraint and decided to kick life into high gear. Why wait when you had been visited by "HOPE" and your paths had been knit together so completely? However, Caleb wanted to give Joy the excitement of a surprise "pop the question" moment. She had helped him beyond belief to find himself and his courage—greater courage than he had ever known. He had never experienced anyone like Joy. He could not wait to spend his life with her. He was grateful to think that someone so wonderful could be utterly in love with him.

Caleb asked her to meet him at a mysterious location according to a map he left in her car. This one was much like the map she had bought just before she saw Hope, her little angel, on the road and had the accident that led her to find Caleb. He had Joy's camera crew hidden out of sight but where they could capture every beautiful moment. Joy arrived and saw the field of sunflowers before she saw Caleb. She began to weep remembering that Hope had told her that she looked like a bright shining sunflower. Joy had kept that moment secret from everyone so she could hold onto that image alone—something reserved for just her and Hope. It made her smile to see such a beautiful shining field of gold, yellow, and orange.

When the love of his life arrived, Caleb was standing in front of a field full of sunflowers with a sunflower bouquet in his hand. Playing in the background was the song "You are my sunshine." He gallantly got down on one knee and asked the question of a lifetime: "Joy, will you be my sunshine for the rest of our lives?" Through tears and screams of joy that could not be contained, Joy and her entire crew screamed at the same time, "YEEESSSSS!!"

This is only . . . **the beginning** . . .